6/2/09

To: Reid,

Best of Luck!

Success By Default
The Depersonalization of Corporate America

by

Best wishes.

Michael Solomon

authorHOUSE™

1663 Liberty Drive, Suite 200
Bloomington, Indiana 47403
(800) 839-8640
www.AuthorHouse.com

First published by AuthorHouse 03/01/05

ISBN: 1-4184-9743-6 (sc)
ISBN: 1-4184-9744-4 (dj)

Library of Congress Control Number: 2004097030

Printed in the United States of America
Bloomington, Indiana

This book is printed on acid-free paper.

This book is dedicated to

HENRY SOLOMON

1918 – 2002

Dad you will always be remembered with a smile.

If you want to see a rainbow,
you must learn to put up with the rain.

TABLE OF CONTENTS

PROLOGUE

There is a superstition called Triskaidekaphobia, it is the fear of the number 13. About 80 percent of all high-rise buildings skip the 13th floor in numbering sequence. Airplanes have no 13th aisle. Many cities do not have a 13th street.

These are things I could never understand because the 13th floor, aisle and street are really there; they just call them something else; 12A or 14.

The Italian National Lottery omits the number 13 from its drawings. The number simply doesn't exist. They don't call it something else.

As you read through this book, you will notice that Chapters Seven and Eleven are left blank. This was not a typographical error, it was done intentionally. This book is about a business success not failure. Never in my business career did I ever want to deal with Chapter Seven or Eleven.   So why start now?

Like the thirteenth floor, which is really there but renumbered, seven and eleven do not exist in this book.

Something of an oxymoron is that in a gambling casino on the crap table seven and eleven can be lucky numbers but not in business.

INTRODUCTION

L et us play a mind game. I will say a word or phrase and you think of a word. *General Motors*. I bet the first thing that popped into your mind was Chevrolet, Cadillac, Pontiac, Oldsmobile or Buick. Let's try another....*Panasonic*. Are you thinking about television sets or stereos? How about, *Baskin Robbins?* Okay, was it vanilla, chocolate or rocky road: with or without the hot fudge?

Do you think you got the answers correct? Well maybe! The one thing that makes all of the above take place you haven't given a second thought. What makes the automobile, television, ice cream and any other product or service on the face of the earth happen is the one thing that gives life to it all, "People."

When you think about a business, what seems to be completely forgotten is that a business, no matter how large or small, is made up of people; people that think, feel and experience all the emotions that everyone does.

The problem as I see it may be that these people are misguided by the rules and regulations they work within, sometimes knowing full well that these rules are questionable; regulations and procedures, which were written by other people. They are just following the rules and when they get treated the way they treat their customers, they don't like it either. Not only are they failing in customer relations, service and business ethics, the executives at the top probably have no idea how bad it can be. They are too busy making the bottom line work so that they can satisfy their stockholders. In trying to keep the investors happy, they many times forget what makes their business run. It is customers. If you don't have customers, you won't have a business.

From the consumers' side, it is probably faster watching grass grow than being caught up in the corporate quagmire of customer service.

I sometimes believe that some businesses live by an eleventh commandant. **When it comes to business the first ten don't apply.**

I found a need to write this book out of frustration in trying to deal with some of the largest corporations in the world.

It has come to my attention that the way to succeed in business is to be yourself, find a niche, create a need, believe in what you are doing, treat your customers the way you would want to be treated, perceive yourself to be different, forge straight ahead, learn from your mistakes and never look back. Better yet learning from the mistakes of others or as I call it becoming successful by default.

To do this without stripping your customers of their dignity and treating them as you would like to be treated is not only an art, but if done correctly is telling your customer that it is your privilege to help them and their right to be helped.

If you are in business and someone calls for service, that is not a problem, it is a customer need. It becomes a problem when you don't handle it correctly.

If you don't take care of your customers someone else will. Further yet, if you don't take care of your employees someone else will.

CHAPTER 1
THE SHIELD

"That's chapter twenty," I bellowed. "What's chapter twenty?" Mary, my office manager, who has been with me for eight years, seemed puzzled. "What are you talking about?" she asked, with some confusion in her voice, as I was hanging up the phone after trying to straighten out a billing problem with our telephone service provider.

"I'm so frustrated; I don't know how these companies stay in business. The biggest companies in the country have the worst customer service departments. I haven't figured it out yet," I said, "but if I was ever to write a book about corporate America this story would be chapter twenty."

I have been in business since 1984; it has been almost twenty years. I have never had an unprofitable year or a day with nothing to do. My success comes not from knowing what to do, but rather in knowing what not to do and remembering the lessons my father taught me about life and how to treat people.

I cannot help but to reflect back to why I have become as successful as I have. The biggest influence in my life was my dad.

Dad wasn't a businessman, or a scholar; he was a simple man who worked as a plumber for a large contractor. But the lessons he taught me cannot be found in books or classrooms. Dad taught me integrity, how to treat people and most importantly how to turn lemons into lemonade. He would say, "You have to look upon life as a barrel of apples, if you want one you have to stick your hand in; you may come up with a rotten one, but if you plant its seeds, you can grow a tree and refill the barrel. If it has a worm in it, take the worm and go fishing." He also taught me to leave some for the little guy. "Don't take all of the apples, leave some for the less fortunate, and only take what you need. Don't be a taker all of your life," he would say. He taught me how to be charitable.

This book is about growing that tree.

It all began in 1981 after a very successful 15 year career with the New York City Police Department. My assignments ranged from a foot patrol in the 9th Precinct in Manhattan to an assignment in the Youth Division less than one year later. After helping the 9th Precinct commander regain control of Tompkins Square Park in the East Village by arresting every offender that came my way and cleaning up the park, he rewarded me with a recommendation for assignment in plain clothes. That's when I joined the Youth Division. I was investigating everything from child abuse to youth gangs, narcotics in schools and one case of incest where the father was having sex with his 14-year-old daughter, while his wife was sleeping with their 17-year-old son and both brother and sister were having sex with each other.

During my tenure in the Youth Division, I was temporarily assigned to the Intelligence Division during the 25th Anniversary of the General Assembly of the United Nations. It was there that I met some of the most powerful people in the world, as part of the security team for the leaders of some of the most powerful countries in the world. I felt proud to represent my country as I stood bodyguard to dignitaries such as the Shah of Iran and Madame Chang of Taiwan.

Right after my assignment in the Intelligence Division, I requested and was granted an interview for an assignment in the Organized Crime Control Bureau as a special investigator. I wanted my detective gold shield so badly, I could taste it. I knew that the fastest way into the detective bureau was through O.C.C.B.

There were two divisions within the bureau. One was Public Morals, which was investigating gambling and vice and the other was the Narcotics Division. I found myself in the latter. When I met with Chief William Boncoue at my orientation meeting, I asked him why I was assigned to the Narcotics Division when I had asked for the Public Morals Unit. He looked me right in the eyes and in front of the whole group of 14 of us said, "Solomon, I read your personnel file, you were hand picked, any other questions?"

The next four years were spent building major narcotics cases and backing up undercover officers. I built up a list of informants some of whom would rat out their own mothers before going to jail. I worked with the lowest of the low, in some of the best neighborhoods in the city. They were so good that when I went home, a hot shower was needed before I would hug our two daughters.

During my tenure in the Narcotics Division, I was considered an expert in drug importation. In 1972, I had attended a two week international seminar in Washington, D.C. with the Drug Enforcement Administration. I had been asked to give the closing remarks at the symposium, which I wrote while driving to the luncheon. I had scribbled some notes on a piece of scrap paper. When it came time to give my remarks, I stood in front of about 120 Police Officers representing departments from all over the world. My stomach was shaking as if I just swallowed a mouth full of marbles and they were bouncing around uncontrollably. Looking poised and confident as though I was presenting the State of the Union Address, I started to speak.

I suddenly remembered my dad's words to me, "When you can't think of anything to say, speak from your heart."

"I would like to talk to you about the Forgotten Victims of Drug Abuse."

I got the idea from a news story on the radio while driving to the meeting. It was about a police officer that was mugged, while off duty, and in serious condition in the hospital.

"There are many victims along the drug trail. When people hear of the victims of drug abuse, their attention automatically turns to the kid who may be shooting himself full of drugs or filling himself up on pills." I paused, took a deep breath and continued. "They and when I say they, I mean the news media as well, rarely give thought to the victims that lie between the drug dealers and those kids. There is little public concern for the police officer who is severely assaulted while working undercover or for the member of an investigating team killed by a trigger-happy suspect with a shotgun."

I was speaking with anger in my voice. I looked out into the audience; I had their complete attention.

"How about the police officer that shoots it out with a robbery suspect trying to get money for his next fix. We seem to get lost in the shuffle and somehow are never regarded as victims of drug abuse. But, I want to tell you that we are and as long as there is a drug problem, we must be considered as victims. When we do become the victim, there is usually no second chance. As Narcotics Officers, we have a tough war on our hands and God only knows if we will win or lose. But win or lose, we are going to put up one hell of a fight."

I went on to say as I lowered my voice. "We have had the financial means and the support of a lot of people for a long time. But now, thanks to the National Training Institute of the Drug Enforcement Administration, we are armed with the most powerful weapon of all – *KNOWLEDGE.*"

My speech was over. It lasted less than two minutes. The applause was thundering, the marbles were gone.

A week later, I received a telephone call from Vince Promuto, the public relations officer of the DEA. (Yes, he is the same Vince Promuto who played football for the Washington Redskins). He said that John Bartels, the Director of the DEA, had heard my remarks and would like to print them in their national magazine. I was flattered and gave them permission. I was a little shocked when I found that they covered the entire back cover of their next edition with my words.

In March of 1974, five months later, at the request of the DEA, I was asked to run a Joint Federal, State and City Task Force as Technical Specialist to do the groundwork for a treaty negotiation between the United States and Turkey. Looking forward to the assignment, I hoped that it might finally get me my detective shield.

My days were spent directing a team of 60 undercover agents who were assigned to buy street heroin. They were making arrests but some of the evidence was sent to a special federal laboratory to do Signature Trace Analysis, the equivalent of DNA Testing, to see if the opium that was transformed into heroin was grown in Turkey. The object was to see if Turkey was adhering to the treaty that they signed in 1969 preventing the farmers from growing the poppy.

Many people don't know it, but those little black poppy seeds on your morning roll or bagel are from the Opium Poppy. Don't worry, even though some of us may be addicted to bagels, I can assure you it has nothing to do with the seeds.

I found myself analyzing the lab reports as they came across my desk, only to realize that the opium content of the street heroin from Turkish sources was higher then believed. In trying to find out why, I read and reread all the intelligence reports I could get my hands on. It was then that I got my first business lesson.

The treaty that was signed in 1969 was for five years. At that time opium was selling for about $40 a kilo. It wasn't that the farmers weren't growing it; they were actually secretly growing it hidden amongst other crops and stashing the opium away waiting for the price to rise. By the end of the fourth year of the treaty, the demand was so high that the price soared to over $100 a kilo. The farmers then took it from their hiding places where it filtered down to the streets of New York and found its way to my desk in the form of a lab report. That was my first lesson in supply and demand.

After that assignment everything that followed seemed mundane. I returned to the daily routine of a Narcotics Officer until 1975, when the budget cuts hit the police department and I found myself back in uniform for the first time in ten years. I was assigned to the 43rd Precinct in the Pelham Parkway section of the Bronx. It was like coming home, since I grew up in that neighborhood and knew almost every shop owner on my beat. There weren't many foot posts anymore. I was lucky. I found myself working 8 A.M. to 4 P.M. Monday to Friday with weekends off, something almost unheard of in the department in those days, still without that gold shield.

Having difficulty making ends meet on a police officer's salary, I enrolled in an Income Tax preparation course in 1973 and began a tax practice to supplement my income. By 1975, I had a client base of over 120 taxpayers.

I re-enrolled in college. Attending the New York Institute of Technology, I was taking 18 credits at night and on weekends while working days. In addition, from January to April, I operated my tax practice. After receiving my Bachelors of Science degree, Magna Cum Laude, I continued on for my Masters Degree and graduated with distinction from Long Island University with a Masters in Public Administration.

I was preparing a tax return for a client during the 1975 tax year, when little did I know that this return was going to be the foundation for changing my direction for the rest of my life. The client who was a police officer had been on disability sick pay for a year. I noticed that the City of New York was deducting Social Security Tax from his sick pay. Believing this to be improper, I started to look into it. Spending hours in the library and talking to other tax accountants, I tried to find a loophole in the law. After researching the tax codes, I discovered that the City of New York was paying Social Security Taxes against sick pay because of a clause in the city's retirement law, which was not necessary to be there. It was like the sun coming out just after a fast moving storm. Everything was suddenly very bright and clear as a bell. The city had been screwing up for the longest time.

The first apple seed was about to be planted.

After almost five years of trying to get the New York City Payroll Department to listen to me, I decided to write to the comptroller directly, even though I didn't believe I would hear from his office either.

On May 19, 1980, I laid out my plan to Harrison J. Golden only to receive a letter from his first deputy, Martin Ives, about two weeks later. His letter was the same as mine only he turned the words around and said that they would have to change one phrase in the current retirement law. Isn't that what I just told you, I thought to myself? If they did that the city would save tens of millions of dollars. But they had no intention of pursuing it at this time.

I was on a one man campaign to get the city to change the retirement law, but no one would listen to me. Even though the comptroller had my plan and knew it was right, he was sitting on his hands.

On July 8th I was in my car listening to a WCBS News Radio 88 Editorial Report. The news editor was expressing concern over where the city was going to get the money to pay for the new municipal, police, fire and sanitation department contracts that were just negotiated. The settlement had averted a strike that was threatened just weeks before.

The more I listened to the report the angrier I became. Here I had the answer; the Comptroller knew it and no one wanted to do anything about it. I thought to myself here's my opportunity. I pulled off the road, found a pay phone, (cellular telephones hadn't been invented yet) and called the radio station. I was put through to Susan Veach, the editorial producer and told her I wanted to reply to the broadcast. Susan asked me what I wanted to say and when I told her, her words were "that's dynamite, put it in writing and get it to me as soon as possible, I can have you on the air by next week."

The following Tuesday I was in their studio recording my concerns. I laid out my plan and quoted the letter sent to me by the Deputy Comptroller. My reply was aired six times on July 16th. As a result of my aired reply on the radio, I was contacted by City Councilman Michael Demarco. Two days later, he introduced me to City Finance Director, Donald Schnakenberg who took my research and said he would get back to me shortly. A week later, I called Donald only to be told that his staff was looking into the matter. He also said that it wouldn't happen for at least a year, if at all, but that he would keep me informed. That was the last time we spoke.

On January 14, 1981 the leaders of the City Council held a news conference to announce that the Council had changed the statute and planned to recover 40 million dollars immediately. The press release said, "The cash windfall, which could be made available almost immediately to help resolve the city's fiscal problems, resulted from a council staff study ordered last June by Majority Leader, Thomas J. Cuite and Finance Committee Chairman, Edward L. Sadowsky. This money represents overpayments by the city to the government's social security program. The council's study and the Corporation Counsel agree that when a municipal employee is logged as being out sick no payment to social security is required. Nevertheless, such payments have been made routinely throughout the 45 year history of the program." Cuite and Sadowsky went on and praised five staff members as having made "a very substantive contribution to the city in a time of great need. They have come up with many millions of dollars – real dollars…the Mayor (Ed Koch) is expected to reflect the savings in his 1982 budget."

If you were to do the math and take into account the increase in the number of municipal employees over the years, you would realize that the City of New York misspent a tremendous amount of money, which totaled in the hundreds of millions of dollars.

I wasn't at the press conference, not that I would have missed it, I wasn't invited. I read about it in the New York Times the next day. They must have spelled my name wrong because when I read the article over and over about four times, I couldn't find it anywhere.

I guess that old saying, "do as I say not as I do," applies to the City Council. As a Police Officer, I was expected to have complete integrity, where was theirs?

I called Susan Veach at WCBS to see if she had heard about the press conference and to, once again, thank her for allowing me to present my plan. She expressed some concern that I wasn't mentioned and didn't know if the station could do anything.

To this day I don't know if she did anything at all, but three days later the editorial pages of the daily newspapers read, "No Reward for Police Officer Who Balanced the City Budget." It was picked up by the wire services and spread like poison ivy.

Even if the City did something for me, the most I was entitled to under the New York City employee suggestion program was a maximum award of $1000. A Detective's Gold Shield would have been nice.

The stories that followed were reward enough. One article said that if I did for the Chrysler Corporation what I did for the city the least I would have gotten was a new car with a trunk full of cash. About a year earlier Chrysler had risen like a Phoenix when the government bailed them out.

I couldn't write that kind of resume. The telephone was ringing off the hook, major corporations and other municipalities were calling and offering me positions in their tax and accounting departments.

I never heard from the City. I felt betrayed. I imagined it was how Caesar felt towards Brutus.

The day the editorials were published I was working my steady post in the Westchester Square section of the Bronx. I walked into the Chase Manhattan Bank to say hello to Darlene Regal the Branch Manager who I was friendly with. She was talking to Steven Klebanoff, a local businessman, who I had met some months earlier. He did his banking there and Darlene had previously introduced us. He was a tall, well-dressed and well-groomed individual that owned a sheet-metal fabrication business. He manufactured air control dampers for heating and ventilating systems. He impressed me because of his manner and accomplishments.

When Darlene noticed me, she got up from her desk, came over and gave me a big kiss on my cheek and said, "Wow, you really did it this time." Steven seemed confused and asked me, "who did you find, Jack the Ripper?" Darlene interjected and said, "You're looking at the man that just balanced the New York City Budget." She then handed him the editorial that was written about me. He quickly read it then shook my hand to congratulate me, and asked, "What could you do for me?" I replied, "Let's talk sometime."

Over the next few weeks, we had lunch a couple of times. Steven laid out his plan for expanding his business and said he needed someone like me to help him with his plans. He wanted to know what my future plans were with the Police Department. I explained that I had six months to go before being eligible to vest my pension and that I couldn't leave until May.

Over the next few months I did some consulting for him and on May 20, 1981 walked into the pension bureau at 1 Police Plaza in Manhattan and signed my retirement papers. I was now the Finance Administrator of Air Balance, Inc., with a package and perks that was worth twice what I had been earning. I had a salary of $35,000, a company car, four weeks vacation, medical and dental insurance, unlimited sick leave and a two year contract which contained a clause that gave me a bonus of three percent of the annual profits of the company.

I never did get my gold shield.

CHAPTER 2
THE DOG AND PONY SHOW

I don't know who was more excited my first day at the office, Steven or me. I was excited and nervous at the same time. This was the real world and I had to perform.

Police work was different, you showed up every day, kept order in your assigned area and hoped that some psycho with a gun wasn't going to try and show you how tough he was. Your workload rarely carried over to the next day.

Now there were projects, reports, collections and a business plan that had to be formulated. My desk was a small conference table that was cluttered with reports and old files. The seat on the motor scooter I sometimes rode as a police officer was more comfortable than the chair I had. Within two months, we had moved the offices two blocks east. I now had my own private office.

With the exception of the office and administrative staff, everyone else was a member of the sheet-metal workers' union. If you ever wanted to stop a union assembly line, all you had to do was walk through a manufacturing plant in a three-piece suit. The office was on the second floor mezzanine with glass windows that overlooked the shop. On a few occasions, I found myself looking out over the plant. Steven had to caution me that the men were suspicious of me if I watched them working. Not that I was spying, I was just interested in the process. My surveillance had to stop.

Steven was friendly with the Union Local president and would, on occasion, meet with him for lunch. During a conversation I had with him after one of his meetings, I became aware of a problem the union was having with the Equal Employment Opportunity Commission. It seemed the union had not been admitting enough minorities and the EEOC was getting ready to come down hard.

One of my first projects was to find financing for a new piece of equipment that we wanted to have custom built. We needed a new sheet steel roll-former with a price tag of $130,000 and I had to find a way to come up with the money.

While researching the opportunities for financing, I found a city agency that was giving low-cost financing tied to expansion. There was one hitch; you had to hire minorities. How can you hire unskilled minorities and have them work side by side with union members. It would only take about two minutes before we would have an immediate strike. But we needed that money.

After some serious self brainstorming, I came up with a plan that just might work. I presented it to Steven.

"The union has a minority problem. We need the money. We start a low wage-training program for minorities and the Local admits them as members under a special training program. If they work out and are still on the program after a year, they are admitted to the union as Apprentices and start to work their way up to Journeymen. The Local will sanction it and it will get them off the hook with the EEOC. Then we get our financing. The bonus is that the first $1,500 of each new employee's salary would be paid for with Targeted Jobs Tax Credits. It is a tax advantage, which is a direct credit of up to $1,500 for each minority that is hired and put into a training program. We could also reduce the cost of the equipment with an investment tax credit of 10%."

"I love it," he replied. "Now I just have to sell it to the union."

The theory with investment tax credits is simple, but, if you listen to liberal economists, it is only a reduction in taxes for the rich businessmen. You get an incentive in the form of a 10% tax credit based upon purchasing new equipment that is designed to help you build a better mousetrap.

Someone has to build that equipment. Someone has to operate it. Someone has to sell the better mousetrap and someone has to buy it. You save 10% in taxes, but you just put 20 more people back to work and the unemployment figures come down. The new products are produced and sold, creating new business, which in turn brings more profits leading to more income tax being paid. Sound familiar; ever hear of *Trickle Down Economics*. Believe me it works.

Steven presented the idea to the Union. It didn't take long for them to give us their blessing; after all we were saving their jobs. Now they had to sell it to the membership and they did. We were one step ahead. I was planting trees all over the place.

I put our new business plan on paper and along with the projected financial statements, applied for low-cost financing from the New York City office of Economic Development. If the loans were approved, we were looking at an 11% payback, which when you consider that the prime rate back then was over 21%, was unbelievably low.

We met with the city representatives about six times. They even came out for a site visit. At one point after a meeting, Steven asked me, "Do you think we will get it?" I said, "It's in the bag, the City owes me one." I wish I felt as confident as I sounded. The most money I ever borrowed was for a $26,000 mortgage on a two-bedroom townhouse in Rockland County that we called home.

About seven weeks after our initial meeting, we were approved for the loan with certain provisions. We had to hire 14 minority candidates, start a training program and meet our projections. We got the money and believe me it had nothing to do with the city owing me.

We started our training program; candidates were coming out of the woodwork. We had to work with community based job placement centers. They sent us the least likely to succeed to interview. Some of the candidates couldn't even speak English and those that could, couldn't read. The ones that could read and speak English couldn't read a ruler, which was something that was required for the job.

It was amazing; all we needed were candidates with three simple qualifications. Willing to work, a brain and the ability to show up. If they had a brain and showed up they weren't willing to work. If they were willing to work and had a brain they didn't show up. If they showed up and were willing to work they didn't have a brain. This was going to be some training program.

After sorting through all of the candidates and picking the most viable, we started them at an hourly wage of $4.50 an hour. The idea was to increase them to $5.00 if they were still there after 90 days and then 25 cents per hour every 90 days thereafter for the first year until they were admitted into the union. We now had lower labor costs; the union didn't have an EEOC problem, but we still had one little problem, which wasn't so little.

The problem was twofold; we had people making $4.50 an hour doing the same work as a union journeyman earning $20.00 an hour. The men making $20.00 an hour were worried that we had men doing the same work as them for $4.50 and the Union sanctioned it. The tension in the shop was like a rubber band stretched to its limit and any minute it was going to snap.

We had to get the union business agent involved to make peace before a riot broke out.

I'm not anti-union. My dad was a union plumber all of his working life. Now being on the side of management, I was looking at the situation from a different perspective.

How do you tell a man, that is threatened by cheap labor, that if you don't have another class of worker and cut your production costs, everyone is going to be out of work soon, even me.

What saved all or us was the fact that the shop steward and union delegate had a lot of respect for the president of the local, who convinced them things would work out and not to make trouble. After all, we saved his job as well.

We managed to get the equipment we ordered and after the usual start-up problems, proceeded with production a few months later.

It was about this time that Steven had met Tom Hill, President of Ruskin Manufacturing Inc., located in Kansas City, Missouri, at a trade show. They started to discuss how their products could compliment each other. Ruskin manufactured air control dampers for heating ventilating systems and we manufactured air control dampers for fire control. Tom's problem was that Mr. Ruskin, who was getting up in years and really did not want to be overly involved in the business, was getting a little cantankerous. Tom needed a way to help him leave with dignity.

Our problem was that we were renting 50,000 square feet of manufacturing space that was underutilized. We also owned a new roll-forming machine that was not being used to its capacity.

What better way then to merge and go public, giving Mr. Ruskin a vehicle out, while at the same time, start manufacturing Ruskin products in New York.

It did not take long before merger talks started.

Now I really had to get to work. Putting together the numbers for our low-cost financing was easy. There was no worry about meeting our projections. All that the city needed was assurance that we would hire a minority quota and pay back the money. I almost got the impression that if we didn't pay it back it wouldn't be a big deal. The only lien the city had was on the new machinery we purchased. What were they going to do with a $130,000 roll-former anyway; put it in City Hall Park for the pigeons to nest on!

This was different, there would eventually be a "Due Diligence" performed and the numbers had better be right.

I started to put everything we were going to need together. I knew there would be an asset evaluation, an audit of our receivables and close scrutiny of our depreciation and amortization schedules.

With my limited accounting knowledge (remember, I was only doing personal income tax returns when Steven met me; I was not an actual accountant), I was doing a great job of winging it over the past eight months, but this was now for real. I started to hit the books to see how we could juice up our net worth. We already had a signed letter of intent in hand so I had to get moving.

I found a little known accounting principle in the Financial Accounting Standards Board called FASB 34, which allowed for the addition of interest owed and paid on an asset purchase that would increase the net worth of the asset. This allowed us to reevaluate the cost of the new machinery to $154,000. This gave us some room in case our inventories came up lower than expected.

The numbers were fairly accurate and the due diligence came out okay. The contracts were signed and we were ready to close, or so we thought.

Little did we know that while we were doing all the negotiating and putting the deal together, old man Ruskin was doing his own wheeling and dealing behind our backs with a company called Philips Industries. Philips was one of the largest manufactured housing companies. With five manufacturing facilities, they were a fortune 500 company with about 300 million dollars in sales.

Steven walked into my office on the Friday before we were supposed to close and said, "Remember the Wizard of Oz?" "What about it," I replied. "We're not going to Kansas on Tuesday, Dorothy." After he explained what had happened we looked at each other. I said, "Who is Philips and where did they come from anyway?" I saw my stock options suddenly disappear like toilet paper being flushed away. It seemed that Mr. Ruskin with 51% of the stock was going to get his way. Besides, who could blame him?

His deal was too sweet to ignore and turndown. But where did that leave us? We had a contract with Ruskin to be bought out.

The dog and pony show worked well. We were ready to rock and roll but someone changed the music.

As it turned out, the deal for Ruskin by Philips was a corporate buyout not an asset purchase, which in reality meant that they were obligated to meet all of Ruskin's contractual obligations. We were one of them. So, we were going along for the ride. Of course Philips wanted to see what they were buying along with Ruskin, so knowing that another due diligence was about to take place, I started to round up the ponies.

Everything went smoothly. A few months later Philips closed with Ruskin. We were scheduled to close the following week. They were buying all of our assets and stock, purchasing our accounts receivables dollar for dollar and taking on our debt. The deal would net us over two times earnings.

The night before we were leaving for Dayton, Ohio to close with Philips, Steven and I were in the office making copies of all the files and records we would need. He was putting together the inventory and equipment lists while I was copying the aging schedule and receivables list. We left the office about 7:00 P.M. and planned to meet in the morning for the flight to Ohio from LaGuardia Airport.

We arrived at the Dayton Airport about 9:30 A.M. with the closing scheduled after lunch. While walking from the Jetway through the terminal, a voice pierced through the hustle bustle of the airport, "Mr. Steven Klebanoff please pick up the nearest courtesy phone." I stood aside while I watched him take a message and then pick up a pay phone next to the one he was using. After about two minutes, he slammed the phone down on the hook with such force you could almost feel the building shake. Before I even had a chance to say a word, he looked at me with his eyes wide open and his face beet red and screamed at me. "Where are the receivables?" I answered, "Right here in my attaché case." He said, "Show them to me." I opened my case and my heart sunk right down to my toes. "You left them on the copy machine." I felt like I wanted to crawl into the nearest hole and disappear. "Ann found them in the copier (Ann was our Office Manager). She's putting them on the next plane and hopefully they will be here before we close."

John Loudin, Philips Comptroller, who we previously met when he was in New York conducting the due diligence, met us at the airport for the drive to their offices. Steven asked him if someone could pick up a package for us that was coming in on a later flight. John said it would be no problem. No way were we going to tell him what it was. We didn't want to look like complete fools, especially me.

We toured their offices and met Bob Brethen, their CEO; Jessie Philips their President and Chairman was not going to be at the closing.

We had lunch with John Loudin. All during lunch, I kept looking at my watch hoping the plane with the receivables list would be on time.

After lunch we went back to the boardroom and proceeded with the closing. Neither Steven nor I said one word about the missing list. By the way, the total receivables that they were buying were about $120,000, one-third of the purchase price. You would think they would have liked to have seen it. The closing went quickly and was over in about half an hour. Just as we were leaving the conference room John Loudin walked in and handed Steven a large manila envelope containing the list. Steven said thank you and we left for our hotel. We were staying over, having dinner at Brethens Country Club and leaving in the morning.

When we got into the taxi to go to the hotel, Steven and I looked at each other and laughed. He was holding the envelope in his hand and said, "What a blunder, they didn't even ask for it."

The next morning we flew back to New York to begin the transition from Air Balance, Inc. to a division of Ruskin, now owned by Philips called Air Balance New York, a solely held subsidiary of Philips Industries, Inc.

We continued our everyday operations. About a month later, we received a call from John Loudin advising that he wanted to come to visit us with some of his personnel administrators (they weren't called human resources administrators in those days).

Steven and I didn't like the sound of this visit.

The morning they arrived, the first thing they did was to lay out the new organizational plan they had developed.

The next thing they did was to terminate half of our administrative staff, even our salespeople. The last people you want to fire is your sales force.

After lunch they left for the airport and went back to Dayton.

To some in business, this is known as Sea Gull Management. The Sea Gulls fly onto the beach, defecate on everything and leave.

I was okay. I still had about eight months left to run on my contract. Besides which, the money I was saving them in taxes was more than my salary and perks.

I pursued a plan to review all of their manufacturing facilities in an attempt to obtain additional tax credits for them. After presenting my plan, Loudin said that they would look into it and get back to me.

About a month before my contract was about to expire, Steven received a letter from John Loudin at Philips. It basically said that I had outlived my usefulness at Air Balance, New York and I could leave or move to Dayton, Ohio where Philips had a position for me as tax administrator.

After dinner that night I told my wife, Barbara, about the situation. I said, "Honey, you are going to love Dayton," to which she replied, "Not like you are going to miss me." I had a choice to make at that moment and it wasn't hard. I never packed.

CHAPTER 3
THE UNICORN

The first morning I awoke without a job, I felt empty like someone drained all the life out of me. I was like a dry lake after six months of no rain. For the first time in over twenty years I was not getting up to go to work. I was frightened; it felt like the first time I took a walk around the corner of the street I was living on. I was about seven years old and when I looked ahead of me nothing looked familiar. I was so panicky and scared that I turned and ran home as fast as I could.

Now, here I was jobless and almost broke. We had very little savings; Barbara was working, but not earning enough to pay the bills. I had a three thousand-dollar bonus that Steven had given me as part of the bonus clause in my contract. Philips let me use the company car for the next 60 days, which meant that I had to buy a car or buy out the company car I was using. I chose the latter, probably because with the prime rate over 18%, buying a new one would have been a financial disaster for us. So I purchased the 1981 Pontiac I was using for less than the depreciated value.

I now had a car, but what about a job. I hadn't had to look for work for over twenty years. I didn't know where to begin and I didn't even have a resume. I didn't know what I wanted to do.

I was always told that I should be in sales because I could sell ice to Eskimos. So I looked for a sales position.

I called a few headhunters and was soon on my first interview with a major printing company.

After my initial interview, with their Personnel Manager, Bill Block, I was called back for a second interview with their Territorial Sales Manager, Sam Kraft. He was a short man about 50 years old, at least 40 pounds overweight and a chain-smoker. He wore a polyester suit and a cheap tie that was not pulled up to his open collar. Later I would learn that he also suffered from angina. When the second interview was over, I said to myself I got the job.

Two days later, I received a telephone call from Sam. He said that they would like to pursue my career path further. He went on to say, "We would like you to be tested by an Industrial Psychologist. We will pay all the expenses."

Three days later, I traveled to Manhattan to be tested.

The receptionist greeted me as I entered the waiting room. After introducing myself, she escorted me to a small conference room. I was seated at a table with ten chairs around it. On top of the table was a small stack of papers that contained the questions from the tests I was told to complete.

I completed everything from a Rorshack Test to the Minnesota Multiphasic Personality Test. You know the test. That's the one that asks true or false questions, like do you still beat your wife? Do you still wet the bed? After about an hour and a half, I was finished.

I then met with Dr. Ingram. As I entered his office, he rose from the large brown leather high back chair he was seated in behind a large oak desk. We shook hands and introduced each other. He was a man about five years older than me, neatly dressed with a blue knit sweater, gray slacks and black loafers.

His office was well-furnished with light green painted walls, a dark green sofa on one side of the room and two overstuffed chairs that matched which were placed perpendicular to the sofa. The walls were covered with diplomas and certificates. I didn't know who he was trying to impress, his patients or himself. Scattered among the framed accolades were a few photographs and prints.

He asked me to make myself comfortable in one of the chairs opposite his desk.

We began with some light conversation about where I had grown up and what schools I attended. He continued with a host of questions, while taking notes on a yellow legal pad that he was holding against the thigh of his crossed legs as he sat and leaned back in the swivel chair.

One of the questions he asked me was, "If you could be an animal what animal would you like to be?" The answer to this question was almost the downfall of my career of selling printing.

I answered, "A Unicorn." When he asked me, why a Unicorn? I said, "I would like to walk down Fifth Avenue during lunch hour so that all heads would turn my way." I guess my answer had a lot to do with my always wanting to be the center of attention. Little did I know that the picture of the unicorn in his office was his way of interpreting my way of trying to win him over by choosing a mythical animal that he liked. I didn't even remember it until I was told about it some weeks later.

During the period between my testing and being offered the position, I would persistently call the sales manager who interviewed me to see if they had made a decision yet.

When they finally offered me the position, I was informed that it was because of my persistence that I got the job. They said they liked that in a person. Sam also told me about the unicorn question and that the psychologist felt that I was trying to win him over with my answer. He also said that the psychologist said that I was not the right person for the job. He believed I was more of a marketing person than a salesperson. He said that I was like the Navy shelling the beach, I could get their attention but the Marines would have to come in to mop up. What he really meant was that I could convince a potential client that he needed our product, but would not close the sale. Baloney, I told myself. What do these guys think, I don't like money? "We are going to take a chance on you," he said.

I started at a salary of $30,000 plus benefits and an expense account. I was given a company American Express Card. After a two week training program, one on one with Sam, I was ready to hit the streets on my own. My office was in Manhattan on the 14th floor of a 30 story office building on the corner of 44th Street and Lexington Avenue. I had a desk and a file cabinet.

My first day in the office I met with Sam. He gave me a list of potential prospects to contact. He said, "This is a list from the salesperson that previously had your territory, see what you could do with it." One company on the list was the New York Telephone Company. He told me, "Don't call on them, it is a waste of time.

He has tried in the past and the purchasing manager would never see him. I even tried myself and couldn't get in the door. I don't know how the name wound up on the list," he said, "but don't call on them."

Part of my duties was to write up a report of all the places I called on during the day and list what my results were. It was a simple form and had room to write my thoughts about the sales call and whether it would be worthwhile pursuing in the future.

What I kept getting drilled into me was that I should make as many lunch dates as possible. It is the best way to sell, I was told. I thought to myself, why would someone want to go to lunch with someone they just met. It should take a couple of meetings first. Why go to lunch and waste the company's money if they didn't have any interest in what I had to say or sell.

But that was the company's way so that's what I did. About once a week Sam would accompany me on a sales call to observe my sales techniques. He always had something negative to say and never complimented me on any of my selling points.

On one particular sales call, I had invited the Purchasing Director from a major prestigious department store to lunch at the Oyster Bar of the Plaza Hotel. Sam was to come along. I was trying to sell them a business return advertising envelope to use with their revolving credit invoices.

We met at the restaurant and I introduced Sam to Jack Dobson, my prospective client. When we were seated, Sam proceeded to remove his polyester suit jacket, loosened his tie, opened his shirt collar, tucked his dinner napkin into his open collar, rolled up his sleeves and lit up a cigarette. I was mortified, like I just got caught cheating on a test. Here I was trying to impress a potential client from an elite department store and my sales manager was acting like a slob. Who would want to do business with us?

The waiter came over to take our drink orders and leave us the menus. Before he could get a word out of his mouth; Sam said in a loud voice, "I'll have a Piña Colada." I wanted to crawl under the table. My sophisticated guest ordered a glass of white wine and I a wine spritzer.

For lunch, I requested a salad and a plain piece of broiled fish. Jack had asked for a salad and grilled shrimp. After Sam finished his second cigarette, he polished off a large appetizer of fried calamari, washed it down with a second Piña Colada, followed by almost half of a loaf of bread with butter.

I was nursing my drink. I am a cheap drunk; one glass of wine and I can sleep all day. When our salads arrived, I used a little oil and vinegar. I don't remember what Jack had on his salad, but my hero and mentor was asking for more Russian dressing and another loaf of bread, while popping antacid tablets like I eat M & M's.

When lunch arrived, my fish was done just right. I asked our guest if his dish was alright,   as Sam was asking the waiter for a side order of French fries to go along with his fried mixed seafood platter.

All during lunch, Sam ate with a lit cigarette sitting in the ashtray beside him; neither Jack nor I smoked. Twice during lunch the waiter came over to change the ashtray for a clean one.

Dessert was the next disaster. Jack and I ordered coffee while my mentor proceeded to ask for cappuccino and pecan pie á la mode. This guy was a walking time bomb. No wonder he had heart problems.

We finished lunch and I told Jack that I would call him in a few days to follow-up on our discussions. As we walked away from the restaurant, Sam started to critique our lunch date. He said that I should learn to be more relaxed, as a potential client feels uptight if I sit there with my jacket on and shirt buttoned up. I guess he never heard that neatness counts.

When he suggested that we catch a cab back to the office, I said that I had wanted to follow-up on a sales lead and would meet him there later. There was no sales lead. I just didn't want to be around him; he made my skin crawl.

A week went by and I called Jack Dobson to see if we could meet and continue our discussions. I never got through to him. He wouldn't take my calls. I didn't have to ask why.

During this time, the breakup of Ma Bell as ordered by Federal Judge Green was in the making. The New York Telephone Company was becoming Nynex. They would need new envelopes by the millions, but I wasn't to call upon them. At least not the New York Telephone Company that was on my call list. But this was Nynex; I decided to go full speed ahead. After all I was the Navy.

I didn't try to make an appointment with their purchasing agent. I wanted to meet with their accounting people to see what they paid for leased warehouse space for their supplies. We had an envelope that was known as a two-way envelope. It was designed to be reused by turning the flap inside out and mailing it back with your payment. Although the envelope was a little more expensive it took up less storage space and freed up one position on an insertion machine.

If they could save on warehouse space by needing less of it and spend less on insertion they could save enough money to make the envelope less expensive, not to mention the savings on postage because the whole package weighed less.

I wasn't trying to sell them an envelope at this point, I was selling a concept. The purchasing agent, as far as I was concerned, usually was instructed in what to purchase and to get the best possible price. I believed I had the best price, not in the cost of the product but in what it could do. The Navy had arrived; the Marines couldn't be far behind.

I kept these sales calls confidential. I didn't want anyone to know that I may have discovered uncharted waters. It worked: I aroused their interest and was to meet with them a week later over a very expensive lunch to hopefully present my plan.

I was extremely excited; I imagined it was how my two daughters felt on their first trip to Disney World.

Now I had to go back to the office and write up my report. If I aroused their interest further and continued to a closing, it would be one of the largest single orders in the history of the branch.

The next day Sam asked to see me in his office. He said, "I read your report. I thought I told you not to call on the telephone company." I said, "You told me not to call on the New York Telephone Company, I called on Nynex." He said, "Don't be a wise guy, what you did borders on insubordination." I felt like a child being scolded for eating all of his dinner. Here I thought I was doing the right thing and he took it as a threat. He could not get to see the purchasing agent and I was about to hopefully write a major order, the first of what could possibility be a long-term relationship.

He said he would have to think about it and would discuss it with me the next day.

The next day, I was told that the account would become a house account and that I would not be servicing them because I was fired.

He asked me for my company credit card. I took it out of my wallet and handed it to him. He took it from my hand and said, "That's not the way you hand in a credit card, you take a scissor and cut it up." I am glad I didn't do that because he certainly would have cited me for destroying company property.

I was in the position for exactly thirteen weeks. I now know how the cast of a sitcom feels when being cancelled.

To this day, I have no idea if they bought the envelopes or my concept. All I know is that when I receive my telephone bill, it is not in the envelope I designed. By the way, I never told him who my contacts were.

CHAPTER 4
THE LOCKER ROOM

It was a long ride home. I took the Metro-North train from Grand Central to the Tarrytown Station where my car was in the commuter parking lot. The forty minute ride seemed like a day. I felt like a butterfly trying to fly against the wind. During the ride, I was trying to figure out my next move. The train was empty, as it was still hours before the daily commuter rush. There weren't many people on the train to distract me. I stared out of the window and watched the boats on the Hudson River. I started to think of where I could find another job.

All kinds of thoughts were dancing in my head. I looked at the seat across from me and saw a newspaper which was folded back to expose a large photo of a sports locker room. That's when it hit me. I'll call Robert.

Robert Strum was the founder of Strum Metals, Inc. The company was located in Astoria, New York. He was in the process of setting up a new business to complement his existing sheet-metal company. He was going to manufacture metal furniture for the sports industry. Their products would include steel lockers for schools and sports centers. He was betting on the health club industry taking off like a rocket ship.

I met Robert when I was working for Steven at Air Balance, Inc. Barbara and I had attended a sheet-metal industry conference in Puerto Rico the previous October. It was actually an industry conference to socialize, network, have a good time and attend meetings and seminars.

Robert was also there. I had met him for the first time and the chemistry was instant.

After five days of sun and fun, we were heading back to the San Juan Airport in a minibus. The last seats were facing each other and Robert moved back to where Barbara and I were seated to face me.

He struck up a conversation and started to ask me all kinds of questions. "What is your background? Where did you go to school? What's your claim to fame?" And the final question, "What do you do for Steven?" I told him about my police career, how I helped balance the New York City Budget and how much I saved Steven in taxes while at the same time helping the Union President, which he already knew.

While I was answering his questions, Barbara's attention was intentionally (she told me later) turned away from our conversation.

On the flight home, she said to me, "I had to turn away. Do you realize that Robert was interviewing you?"

I said yes, but I wouldn't leave Steven. Besides, he didn't make me an offer. Boy, do I need him now. I said to myself, as soon as I get home I will call Robert and maybe he'll make me that offer.

I called him only to find out that he wasn't in. I left a message for him to please return my phone call. I found out later that evening, when he called me back, that he was calling from his room in a hospital where he was being tested for stress and exhaustion. Nobody was to know, not even me, but he really had a heart attack. "What are you up to?" he asked. "I'm ready to make a career move," I replied.

"I could use someone to run the financial end of my new business; you'd be perfect. What are you looking for?" "What are you offering?" I asked. I was trying to make him believe that I was bargaining from strength, but I didn't want this to turn into a poker game; I'll see your five and raise you ten.

"Give me a number where I can call you back tomorrow," he said. "I'd rather call you. I don't want anyone at work to get suspicious," I replied. "Okay, call Evelyn in the morning."

My dad always said, "Always show them you're strong never show your weak side."

Evelyn Gurlock was his comptroller and assistant. She was a woman about 45, divorced, about five feet four inches tall and weighed about one hundred pounds soaking wet. As a matter of fact every time I saw her, she looked sickly. The first time I met her was on the trip to Puerto Rico. Her skin was so pale that it looked as though someone had drained half of her blood. She was a workaholic; in at 8:00A.M. and didn't leave until at least 10:00 P.M. Everywhere that Robert went, she was right by his side. He didn't make a move without her. I sometimes wondered who owned the businesses Robert or Evelyn. It didn't make sense to me.

I called her about nine the next morning. She was expecting my call. "Robert told me you would be calling. He wants me to set up a meeting as soon as possible. When can you come in?" "How's

Wednesday?" I asked. "Ten o'clock," she replied. "No problem I'll see you then."

Wow! That went smoothly, I told myself. I felt a little nervous about the meeting, but at the same time a little relieved. I was certain that they would make me an offer. I didn't want to seem too anxious, but at the same time I needed a job. There is a certain comfort level taking a position where you know the firm and the people who are going to employ you.

The Wednesday morning drive from Rockland County was a little slow. It had been raining. I left early in case there was traffic during the 40 mile trip and arrived at their offices about 9:45 A.M. with a few minutes to spare.

I announced myself to the receptionist, an attractive young woman about 25, who had long dark hair and hazel eyes. I couldn't tell how tall she was because she was sitting behind a high reception desk. Her name was Judy. What I didn't know was that she was only filling in for the regular receptionist who was going to be late due to the weather. The other thing I didn't know was that she was going to be my assistant if I accepted an offer.

"Ms. Gurlock is expecting you. You can go right in. Her office is the last door on the left down the hall." "Thank you," I replied. I turned and walked down the corridor. Each office I passed on the left had glass partition walls that you could see into as you walked past. Evelyn's office, however, was the only one with solid walls. It was right next-door and perpendicular to Robert's. I approached her office, peeked in and gently knocked on the open door. It was 9:55 A.M. She was on the phone and motioned for me to come in and have a seat on an upholstered chair that was placed in front of her desk. Her office was cluttered; there were piles of papers and folders all over the place. There was a credenza behind her desk that seemed to be playing hide and seek with the amount of papers and folders that were on it.

She was obviously talking to Robert, because her last sentence was, "He just arrived and I will call you when we are through." She hung up and started to rise from her chair. I immediately stood up and extended my hand. I could feel the bones in her hand that were covered by a thin layer of skin. I was afraid to grip her hand too hard for fear of breaking her fingers. "How are you?" I said. "Fine," she replied. "And you?" "I'm good." Not really, I thought to myself. I really need this job.

"That was Robert on the phone. We had discussed you in length. He would like to have you take over the financial administration of the furniture side of the business. He needs you to straighten it out. It's a mess. When are you available?"

Whoa, slow down a little, I thought. I need to digest what has just happened here. Somewhere, someone forgot to ask questions. Usually in an interview there are questions. This wasn't an interview. I wasn't sure what it was. She was talking to me as though I was already on the payroll and they were promoting me to another position.

"I won't be available for at least ten days." I wanted her to believe that I was still employed.

"What are you making now?" Zero, but you're not going to hear that from me lady. "I'm earning thirty-three thousand dollars a year. In addition to that I am receiving three weeks vacation, family medical and a monthly car allowance," It was actually thirty thousand, two weeks vacation, medical, but no car allowance. I was bluffing. I kept my poker face intact. After what just transpired, I was certain that she wasn't going to check. Besides she didn't even ask me where I was working.

"What if we offered you thirty-seven, three weeks vacation, medical and a one hundred and fifty dollar monthly car allowance?" she asked.

I'll take it, I thought, but the words never came out of my mouth. "Can I think about it and let you know tomorrow?" "Alright, you can call me in the morning."

It was 10:10 A.M. and the interview was over. I was on my way home with an offer in my pocket. I felt excited like I just found a fifty dollar bill in an old pair of pants that I didn't know was there.

I called Evelyn the next morning to tell her I would accept their offer. "That's great, Robert will be happy," she said. "When can you start?" "How about a week from Monday. I want to give my employer at least a weeks notice." "Okay we'll see you then," she replied.

It has always amazed me how through this entire process I was never asked one question relative to my previous employment or anything related to my abilities. I still wonder to this day if I was that good or did I just pull off the biggest hustle of my career.

A week from the following Monday I arrived at the office by 8:30 A.M. I didn't want to be late my first day. Evelyn was already there. After filling out the usual employment, payroll and insurance forms, she escorted me to my office. It really wasn't an office. The administrative side of the offices was a wide-open loft area. The desks were makeshift with a door being held up on both ends by two filing cabinets. I was lucky I had a desk and credenza. This meant that I had two doors and four filing cabinets, which I sat between.

Evelyn then introduced me to Judy, who when we last met was sitting behind a reception desk. I shook her hand and said, "You surprised me. I thought you were the receptionist." "No," she replied. "I was just filling in." "Why don't you show Mr. Solomon around and introduce him to everyone," Evelyn said. "When you're done, come back to my office and we'll get started on what we need to accomplish."

I followed Judy down the stairs to the first floor where the operations and manufacturing facilities were located.

Judy introduced me to Nick Lester who was the production manager. He was about 50, close to 5'10", graying hair and a trim build. "I'm glad to meet you," he said, "I've heard a lot about you." "Thanks," I said, "I'm glad to be aboard." "You've got a hell of a job ahead of you. This place is a mess. I hope you can straighten it out." "I'll give it my all," I said. "We should have lunch, I can fill you in on some of the problems," he added. "Let's do that," I replied as Judy and I started up the stairs.

When we reached the second floor, Judy turned right into our office and I went left to Evelyn's. "Come in; I want to tell you what needs to be done. There is a lot of accounting that needs to be followed-up on. The books are not complete at all and they should be brought up to date. Judy knows where all the files and invoices are and she can help you get started." "Alright," I said.

51

"We should meet often until you understand how we do things here," she added.

I went back to my desk and asked Judy to fill me in on where I could find the necessary files and books that I needed. She said it's all here and opened two file drawers full of invoices, most of which had not been paid nor even entered into a journal. "Is there a set of books," I asked. "If there is, I haven't seen them," she answered. "Most of this stuff goes back to when we started keeping records which was about seven months ago. None of it has been posted anywhere as far as I know." "Who did the books before I got here?" "Evelyn did, but there were no books. She only had me file these bills away and paid what needed to be paid when the vendors screamed for money."

I started to think to myself that this sounds like this place is flying by the seat of its pants. Boy have I got my work cut out for me.

I purchased a ledger and journal from our stationery supplier and started to create a set of accounting records. Judy did not have many bookkeeping skills, so I really couldn't rely upon her. I had to instruct her on how to write up a journal and we finally got started trying to get everything up to date.

The fifth week I was there, Evelyn called me into her office and told me that I was to fire Judy. "Why? What's the reason?" I asked. "I can't go into it just yet, but she has to go. Robert wants her out of here by Friday," she added. "If you don't feel comfortable with it, I'll do it myself. Tomorrow the two of you come into my office about four and we will take care of it."

I was having trouble sleeping that night knowing what was about to happen the next day. I had no idea what was going on. She was doing a decent job for someone with limited knowledge of bookkeeping and I couldn't understand why she was being terminated.

About four the next afternoon my phone rang, it was Evelyn. "Why don't you and Judy come to my office and we will take care of what we have to do." "We," I thought to myself. What's this we? I have nothing to do with this. I like the girl; she's bright, shows up and willing to work.

"Evelyn wants to have a meeting," I said as I hung up the phone. "Let's go to her office." As we walked down the corridor, it seemed like a mile even though it was only about sixty feet long. My stomach was in knots; it was doing flip-flops like I was riding a roller coaster. We walked into her office. "Close the door," she said." As I turned to close the door, Judy was starting to sit down. Before her back came to rest on the back of the chair the words were out of Evelyn's mouth. "We are letting you go." Again with the "we"! Hey lady I'm not part of this, I thought, so what's with this we.

Judy's mouth hung open, her lip started to quiver as she tried to speak. When she seemed to regain her composure, with tears welling up in her eyes, she said, "You're just doing this because of Donald. This has nothing to do with my work." "No," was Evelyn's answer, "it has nothing to do with that, you are too young for the job. We are looking for someone with more maturity." It's a good thing this didn't happen ten years later. She could have been sued for a statement like that. Too young for the job, why did you hire her in the first place, I thought.

"You can say what you want, I know differently," Judy replied. "We want you to part on good terms; however this will be your last day," said Evelyn. I felt sorry for Judy. It was almost like it was me that was being fired. Judy got up and started for the door, "I know you had nothing to do with this," she said to me, but be careful," she added. "They will throw you out just as fast and they don't need an excuse." She left the office with tears running down her cheeks.

I said to Evelyn, "Who is Donald and what does he have to do with her dismissal?" "Donald is Robert's nephew. They are dating and he works in the operations office. Robert wants to break it up, so I had to get rid of her."

So here I was without an assistant. Evelyn said to call a temp agency and get a temporary bookkeeper. So that's what I did. After going through three temps, I finally got someone that could do the job. We were able to get the books written up and balanced, but the business was still flying by the seat of its pants. I felt like a loose button being held on by one last thread, any minute I was about to fall off.

I was doing the entire accounting and recordkeeping for the business. I seemed to be putting out more fires than anything else.

Vendors kept calling for payment only to be told that a check went out weeks ago. Unknown to me was the fact that I prepared the checks and gave them to Evelyn to be signed and mailed and it never happened. This was the pattern I soon found out. There was little or no money in the business account. Funds would be borrowed from one of the other businesses to pay bills that were needed to keep vendors off of our backs. The piles of papers that were on the credenza in Evelyn's office were nothing more than checks clipped to invoices marked paid but never left her office.

Vendors checks being withheld wasn't as bad as her not paying such items as sales tax and employee withholding taxes. I couldn't believe how we kept functioning.

Nick would complain that he didn't have raw materials to meet our delivery dates. Steel suppliers would cut us off for non-payment. Paint and hardware suppliers did the same. He would make up a list of materials we needed to meet our numbers. They would be purchased through one of the other businesses and moved into the new manufacturing areas.

Nothing was getting done. It amazed me how this place stayed afloat. We were robbing Peter to pay Paul; only Peter didn't have enough to borrow, so we just kept using credit lines from various sources. It was so frustrating that I was feeling pressure all around me.

After a few weeks, I lost my temporary bookkeeper. She left for a better position. There was an employment agency we were using for other administrative help, so I started to interview for an assistant. After several candidates, I found one woman that seemed to fit the position. I met with Evelyn and asked if she wanted to meet her. "No reason to if you like her that's good enough for me," she replied. So I offered the candidate the position.

She was a woman about 30 years old, not very attractive, and about 80 pounds overweight. When Evelyn met her for the first time about three days later, she said that she would like to see me in her office. When I walked into her office she asked, "Why did you hire her? She's too fat. Don't you know that fat people are out sick more than others?" "You said to hire whomever I liked, that I would have to work with them and it didn't matter to you. Besides she is more qualified than any other candidate interviewed. I don't judge people by what they look like; I judge them by whether or not they can do the job."

My dad always would say, "Never judge a book by its cover." Why was this any different, I asked myself.

"But I didn't think you would hire a fat person, you should know better than that."

I suddenly felt that nothing I did was ever going to be right. It was either her way or no way. This woman has too much power, I thought. How can I do my job if everything I do is being questioned? I wasn't the only one to feel this way. Discussions I had with managers in some of their other offices felt the same way about her. It's her way or the highway, they would say.

I was so uptight that my frustration was leading to anxiety. I would come to work with knots in my stomach. I was being treated like a dog that misbehaved and was constantly being beaten with a newspaper. It got so bad that the thought of going into the office while she was there would actually make me regurgitate. I was getting sicker and sicker. I was working about ten hours a day, six days a week with nothing to show for it but frustration, anxiety and the start of an ulcer.

"I've got to get out of there," I told Barbara. "So start looking for another job," she said. "I am going to," I responded.

The very next day I walked into my house carrying a cardboard box. Barbara asked, "What's in the box?" "Personal effects, I got fired." "What happened?" "She called me in and said they didn't like my management techniques, so they are letting me go. You know what, as soon as she said that, the pain in my stomach went away."

"I guess Judy was right." "Right about what?" she asked. "It doesn't matter," I replied.

I started believing that there was something wrong with me. I have had three positions in the last year and a half. All I wanted to do was use my style, apply my dad's lessons and manage. I can do it and I am good at it.

So what's wrong with people?   I was having a personal pity party and it was not doing me any good. I lost my desire to function.

Air Balance: I can understand, there was a buyout and they were cleaning house. It had nothing to do with my performance. Besides, they wanted me in Ohio. It was my choice not to go.

The sales job: I had a sales manager who was an egomaniac. I believe I made him look bad when I was ready to sell to the telephone company and he couldn't even get a foot in the door.

This last position: I am not sure of. I couldn't figure her out; I believe to this day she was a control freak.

If this wasn't the greatest lesson in how not to treat people than nothing was.

CHAPTER 5
AMWAY

I was so depressed that I couldn't function. I would stay in bed for hours. This lasted for about two weeks until I got up one day and realized that my behavior was totally unproductive.

I went through the New York Times employment section looking for another job. I read an ad for a position as a salesperson for a company that was opening up a new territory in the New York area. I didn't recognize the area code but called the number anyway. The person I spoke to seemed pleasant. He asked me what I had been doing. I explained that I had some sales experience and that I was retired from the New York City Police Department. He sounded very excited when I told him I was a former police officer. It was then that he said, "I would love to have you come in for an interview. The product we are distributing is a security product and as a retired cop it would be right up your alley. We want to set up an office in New York. You could make a lot of money, I'm sure," he added.

Their office was in Westfield, Massachusetts. We set up an appointment for the next morning at 10:00 A.M. I was given directions and was excited about the interview.

I left at about 6:30 A.M. the next morning for the two and a half-hour drive. I didn't want to be late.

About 70 miles into my trip I ran into a blinding snowstorm that practically crippled the road. Traffic was moving at a snail's pace. I could hardly see the road in front of me. There were cars pulled off the road all over the place, but I had to keep going. I was starting to feel anxious as the time was passing.

By the time I got to the Massachusetts border of Connecticut it was almost 10:00 A.M. I pulled into a gas station, found a pay phone and called the person I was going to see.

"Good Morning, this is Michael Solomon. I must apologize; I know we have a 10:00 appointment, but I ran into a major snow storm and I am going to be late. I am about twenty miles away." The voice on the other end of the telephone said, "Hey if you can't get here on time why don't you just forget it." I was so angry. I nearly killed myself getting this far and he was calling it off. I couldn't let him do this to me. I started to explain, "I am sorry, but I left with plenty of time to spare. I just drove 120 miles in a snowstorm to meet with you. I could have turned around, but I didn't. I pulled over to call you from the first telephone I found to apologize. Now you are telling me you don't want to see me because I am going to be late due to a condition that is beyond my control." I was begging. When I think of this now I feel sick that I would stoop so low, but I wasn't going to turn around now. I came this far and I was not going home without this meeting. "Alright you can come in for the interview. Make sure you are here within one hour. I won't wait any longer." "I'll be there," I said.

The hazardous weather driving school I attended in the police department finally paid off. I made it to their office with about ten minutes to spare.

It was a two-story office building. The person I was seeing occupied an office on the first floor. When I entered through the wooden door, I was shocked to find a very sparsely furnished office. It was about 200 square feet. It contained one desk, one file cabinet, a love seat and three folding chairs. I can't remember the name of the company. I filled out an application, which asked for my name, address, telephone number and social security number and nothing else.

The product was an ultrasonic sound detector about the size of a clock radio. It was designed to give off a loud piercing sound when it detected noise. It was used to frighten intruders.

It was explained to me that this was a multi-level marketing product and I was to find other people who wanted to carry the product. I would receive a percentage of what other people sold and I could keep all the profits on what I sold.

This is what I drove 140 miles for and almost getting killed doing it. Amway! Not me, I said to myself. The entire interview lasted about 30 minutes. When I left, I got into my car, drove about 100 feet in the parking lot, pulled over and started to cry. I felt beaten, betrayed and helpless. Thank God I didn't have a gun with me. I probably would have ended it right there.

I don't know how I got home; it was a complete blur. All I know is when I arrived I cried uncontrollably for about an hour. Barbara thought I was having a breakdown. So did I. I can never remember feeling so depressed in my life.

I lied down on our bed and fell asleep on top of the covers with my clothes on, but it wasn't restful. I remember hearing my dad's words over and over as I tried to sleep. "If you get a rotten apple plant the seeds." I have had more rotten apples in the past two years than I ever wanted. So now what do I do? I kept thinking back about my life. Why did I ever leave the police department? It was safe. You went to work every day, you didn't have to answer to too many people and you got a paycheck every two weeks. There is something that has to be said about working for the city.

CHAPTER 6
THE MATRIARCH

As I fell deeper into sleep and started to dream, I remembered my grandmother's words: "Get a civil service job; you will always make a living." She was the matriarch of the family and ruled it with an iron hand. She was a painting contractor, the only female business owner in the painter's union. My grandfather and uncle were her only painters except for an occasional helper or two.

Besides my uncle, there were two daughters, my mother and her older sister. Max, my dad's older brother, was my aunt's husband. Simply put, two brothers married sisters.

We were three families living in one big single-family house. Each family had their own bedroom. I was the oldest grandchild. I was born an Aries in March of 1944, one-month after my uncle landed with the U.S. Navy in Europe as a sailor on an LST troop carrier. My grandmother used to say that my being in the house was the only thing that kept her sanity. It took her mind off my uncle who was 4,000 miles away.

Dad was working in the Brooklyn Navy Yard as a steamfitter. His punctured eardrums prevented him from enlisting into the Armed Services. Mom never worked and along with my grandmother tended to my needs.

Eighteen months later my aunt gave birth to a son. Three years later my aunt and uncle divorced. That's when living under one roof became stressful. As young as I was, I can still remember the words I heard when the conversation turned towards my uncle. He was never called by name, but my dad was becoming known as "His". It was always, "His brother" not Max. My mother would never visit my dad's parents. Probably because "his brother" might be there. So I would visit with my dad alone.

Dad and I would ride the IRT Subway together from the Bronx to East New York, Brooklyn. I can still remember stretching up to try to reach the white porcelain handholds. I would stand on my toes trying desperately to reach them. I was still about a foot short. Dad would hold me up so that I could wrap my little hand around one and hold on. He would say, "Someday you will be tall enough to reach them yourself." I couldn't wait for that day.

I do not know how old I was when it happened, but at some point in my young life, I stopped visiting my paternal grandparents. Not because I didn't want to make the trip, but because my mother didn't want me to go. I know it was not her doing but her mother's idea. It always appeared to me that my mother didn't have a mind of her own. Whatever the matriarch wanted she got.

When I was about eight years old, we moved up the street to a three story walk-up apartment. We lived in a one bedroom apartment. I almost had my own room; it was a bed in the alcove of the kitchen. We lived there for four years until my grandmother sold her house and purchased a two family house three blocks away that we moved into with her. Here we were three families together once again. Only this time, we had our own apartment. I still did not have my own room; I shared one with my sister, who was four years younger than me.

I never saw much affection between my parents. Much of this was probably due to the fact that my mother was never home. She would spend all day with my grandmother upstairs in her apartment, come home for dinner and return in the evening. She couldn't leave her mother's side.

Many of the happy times I remember were the times I spent fishing with my dad. Dad taught me to fish when I was just five years old. I loved spending time with him. We would spend weekends together, before the summer season, at a lakefront bungalow we owned in Middletown, New York.

I remember driving into town with him in the evenings to go to the movies. They still had double features in those days. I can recall the first 3-D movie I ever saw which was *Creature of the Black Lagoon.* I was so frightened that it was a week before I would go near the lake. I guess it was like not wanting to take a shower after seeing Alfred Hitchcock's *Psycho.*

It wasn't until my Bar Mitzvah that I was reacquainted with my dad's parents once again. I can still remember the arguments my parents would have about my celebration. My mother didn't want to invite my dad's parents or any of his three other brothers. Imagine not having half of your grandparents and uncles at your Bar Mitzvah.

Dad won out, but the party was like a high school dance with the girls on one side of the room and the boys on the other. It was the Hatfields and McCoys, only no one had guns. The evening was strained to say the least.

I remember opening the many gifts I received. One gift I opened was from my maternal grandparents. It was a five hundred dollar U.S. Savings Bond.

Thirty years later, during an argument with my mother, I found out that the bond I received from my grandmother was really money my mother skimmed from my dad's paycheck each week. She put the money in an "E" bond and had my grandmother give it to me disguised as a gift. She said, "I wanted you to have it in case your father and I got divorced, you would have some money to help raise your sister." Did she really think that five hundred dollars would go a long way? "So this means that my grandmother never gave me a Bar Mitzvah gift." "That's not true," she said. "Then what do you call it," I countered. She never answered.

As time went on, I became closer to my dad. It wasn't anything big that brought me nearer; it was the little things, like traveling to Peekskill, New York on weekends in the spring. My dad had a side job working on summer rental vacation homes for his cousin. He would do plumbing and I would help him by handing him tools and parts. In the late afternoon, we would go fishing at nearby Lake Oscawanna.

We would talk for hours. He would tell me stories about life on his parent's farm in Parksville, New York, where he grew up; about all the cows they had, making maple syrup, growing pumpkins, corn, tomatoes and everything else you can imagine.

Dad was the only person I know that took three years of Latin in high school. He could have entered any college he wanted

71

to, but didn't go because he had to take care of the family farm after his dad took ill.

He always looked at life with the glass half full not half empty. If it rained and I was disappointed that we couldn't go fishing, he would say, "Just wait, the fish bite better after it rains." He was right.

He was very profound in his thinking. He would say, "Not making a decision is a decision not to make one."

He taught me doing a little the right way was better than doing more the wrong way. "One drop of oil in the right place is better than two alongside," he would say.

We were a team; we did everything together.

My parents separated in November of 1965, six months after I married Barbara and two months after my sister's wedding.

I was restless during my broken sleep. I could feel Barbara gently removing my shoes and covering me with a blanket. I was frightened; I was so depressed that I didn't want to wake up. In the background, almost through a haze, I heard her say to one of our daughters, "Daddy's sleeping; don't go in our room." I was tossing and turning, not on the bed, but in my mind. I felt as though my head was caught in a tornado twisting and spinning out of control.

I was ready to quit. Thoughts of suicide kept running through my mind, the emotional pain was too much to bear. I had no strength left. It seemed like I was running out of options. I felt trapped like a rat in a corner. The only difference is that cornered rats fight back and I didn't want to fight any longer.

I must have fallen deeper into sleep because I did not remember feeling depressed any longer, but I kept dreaming.

It was like watching a movie about my life. I dreamt about my four and a half years in high school. Why wasn't I a better student? If I studied harder then I wouldn't have had to go back to college years after we were married. I could have chosen a different path in life, maybe become a lawyer or other professional.

I thought about the jealousy I used to feel towards our friends who were professionals and the same age as me. Their income levels were three times what I was earning. I wanted more.

So now what? Do I lay here and feel sorry for myself or do I get up and do something about it?

I awoke the next morning feeling washed out, but with a new sense of what I needed to do. First, I have got to stop feeling sorry for myself and kick this depression; next, I have to make a real effort to find a good job.

The following week I managed to secure three interviews. One was with a major insurance company as a fraud investigator, the second was with the Essex County, New Jersey Department of Probation as director of their probation department and the third interview which really got me excited.

It was a large residential and commercial security systems installation company. They were looking for a general manager and financial director; they said that they liked my resume. The company also offered dealerships to anyone who wanted to enter the business.

On the second interview, the personnel manager told me that they were very interested in me and would like to make me an offer. He further explained that the company was very liberal with their benefits package and believed that if they kept their employees happy, they and everyone else benefited in the end. They offered me $55,000 a year plus benefits. The salary was almost one and a half times what I had been earning in my last position. I asked him about a contract, "not a problem," was his reply.

I asked if I could see their financial statements. I wanted to see the company's growth over the years. More importantly, I wanted to see if they could afford to hire me.

Not only did I get a copy of their financials, I was also told that their sales were expected to triple within the next two years as the security industry was booming. Along with the financials, they gave me a marketing research study on the industry to read. It was Friday; I told them that I would like to think about their offer over the weekend. "Take your time," he replied, "we will talk on Monday."

CHAPTER 7

This chapter intentionally left blank.

CHAPTER 8
GOING IT ALONE

I was excited about the offer, but didn't want to jump in with two feet until I had a chance to read the literature I was given.

Halfway through the marketing studies, the words recurring revenue kept jumping into my mind. Ongoing receivables just for servicing alarm systems. Every security system should be connected to a central station that will monitor the alarm and notify the proper authorities. That's the recurring revenue; monthly fees for monitoring alarm systems.

Along with the marketing study was an article from a trade magazine that spelled out how in the security industry it was as simple as installing 15 systems a month for ten years and you could bank one million dollars. It sounded too good to be true. Usually, if it is too good to be true it is. Not the case in this industry.

I made my decision over that weekend. I was going to turn down their offer and go into business.

Part of my decision was something I had learned growing up. After my aunt and uncle divorced, every time I had received a gift, my grandmother would buy the same gift for my cousin. I remember her words to this day, "you have a father to help you out; he doesn't." I recall receiving a portable radio as a Bar Mitzvah present from my aunt. (At the time portable radios were about the size of a shoe box and operated on batteries that totaled 90 volts.)

After I received my gift, my grandmother bought the identical radio in a different color for my cousin. It seemed that if I saved any money from working after school or receiving my allowance and bought myself something, my cousin was rewarded with the same item, only I worked for mine he didn't.

The straw that broke the camel's back, the one that really taught me to fend for myself, was my first new automobile purchase. From the time I was about 14 years old, I always dreamt that when I was older I would buy my own new car. I worked after school delivering groceries, awoke at 5:00 A.M. on the weekends to caddy on Pelham Golf Course and had a small newspaper delivery route. I worked summer jobs as a messenger and mailroom clerk in the city. I did everything possible to make my dream of a new car come true. By the time I turned 19, I had managed to save $2,400, just

enough to purchase a 1964 Chevrolet Impala. I was $125 short for the option of an automatic transmission, so I settled for a stick shift. I didn't want to wait any longer. The night I went to buy my dream car, the whole family was there; grandparents and all. I placed my order and my dad signed the usual papers for me (legally you had to be 21 years old to purchase a car back then, so it had to be in his name).

I was excited. I was so happy. It was hard to believe that all those years of hard work finally paid off. I was like a kid with a giant helium balloon bouncing it around and around.

Unfortunately, the balloon was about to deflate. My grandmother turned to my grandfather and said, "What do you think…. should we buy another car?" It wasn't a question, it was a statement. The next thing that happened was that my grandmother placed an order for a car in the same color, only this one had t automatic transmission. "He doesn't know how to drive a s shift," she stated.

So they bought my cousin a new car which he was a surprise a month later when he returned from college af school.

i

r

*b*o

$1,

So the lesson I learned was that if I wanted something badly enough, I would have to do it myself, was starting to take hold once again.

I wanted that big payoff; I was going for broke, I wanted all the marbles, and I didn't want an apple, I wanted a tree. I was ready to plant another seed.

On Monday I called the director of personnel and asked if I could explore the possibility of becoming a dealer. "Sure," he said, "we are always looking to expand our dealership program. Why don't I set up a meeting for you with our dealership director and you can discuss it with him." "Fine," I said. Three days later I met with Sam Daley and found out that all it took was $8,000 and a dealership agreement and I would be in the security alarm business. The money included marketing and sales literature, a four-day training course on installation and sales plus enough security equipment to protect eight homes.

Based on what I should charge for the installation of each system, I should turn my $8000 investment into about $13,000 in about four weeks. Not a bad return on my investment if I could do . Besides the profit on the installation, I would get eight recurring venue accounts that would pay me $20 a month each. That was the us, for every eight systems I installed I would earn an additional 20. a year. You don't have to be a math major to realize that if I

installed two systems a week, not only would I earn a profit on the installation, but by the end of the first year my recurring revenue income would be over $24,000 and could only grow from there.

I made up my mind I was going to do it.

But before I started, I had to have a business plan. I had to explore the industry locally and find out as much as I could about it. Not the installation of the equipment, but the marketing and sales end.

I looked through the local yellow pages and found that it contained over forty companies in the alarm installation business. So I picked the largest ads and made appointments to have my home surveyed for a system. I asked for a salesman to come over and give me a proposal.

Of the fifteen phone calls I made, six companies never called me back. The nine that did call back, made appointments to come to my house. Only three people actually showed up; two called to say they couldn't make it and that I should call them back in a few days to reschedule and the other four never showed or called at all.

The three estimates I received ranged from $1,600 as the low to $3,300 as the high. All three bad-mouthed their competitors with horror stories about how they wreak havoc in people's houses. They were hacks that didn't know what they were doing.

I told all three companies that I would like to think about it for a few days and thanked them for their time. To this day (and it is twenty years later) none of them called me back to follow-up.

I now had my business plan in place. The following weekend, I was at the community swimming pool where I saw four couples who we were very close friends with. I announced that I was going into business and what I was going to do. One said "You are going to need insurance. I work for an insurance agency. Call me for your insurance needs." Somewhere in his words I didn't hear congratulations or good luck.

Another voice said, "Do you know how many companies there are in that business in the county? There must be at least twenty-five," she said. "No there are forty-seven," I answered. "You really think you can make it in business with all that established competition?" another voice countered. "Yes I can," I said, "I have a business plan, they don't." "What's that?" someone asked. "It's simple, I'm going to do two things, call people back and show up."

Now I had another reason to do it on my own. I was going to prove to my friends that they were wrong.

I needed a name for my business and researched all the business names from the business register in town hall. The name I chose was available and was the one I really wanted: *Pro-Tech Security Systems.* I filed my application to operate a business under that name. I was now officially in business.

I completed the dealer application forms and before long I was traveling to Charlottesville, West Virginia for training.

When I arrived home from training, I was greeted with nine boxes of security equipment that UPS had delivered. I carefully separated each piece of equipment and stored them in a basement closet that I had set aside for my inventory.

My first office was a desk that not only was used for my new business, but also contained my income tax practice that I was still operating. It was located in a six by nine storage room in the corner of my basement. There were no windows in the room. The only difference between my office and a jail cell was that this room didn't have bars.

So here I was in business for myself. Even though I had a business plan, calling people back was the easy part; getting them to call you first was the one thing I forgot to include in my plan.

I proceeded to let everyone I knew know that I was in the security alarm business. I would cold call every business owner that I could cover each day that didn't have a security system in his or her place of business.

Slowly things started to evolve. The first system I sold was to an acquaintance of mine who was also a tax client. It took me two days to install the system. I netted almost $800 in profit, which was equivalent to two weeks take home pay from my last job.

The next week, I cold called an insurance agency. I had walked into an office to see if they had a system. When I introduced myself to the receptionist, the president of the company was standing there; he introduced himself to me; "Hi, I'm Charlie Fritz, president of the firm." I extended my hand and replied, "Michael Solomon, President of Pro-Tech Security Systems, I would like about two minutes of your time. I have a plan that would save your clients money and not cut into your commissions." "Why don't you come into my office and talk to me," he said. I felt like my ship had just come in. Getting in with an insurance broker would be absolutely unbelievable. Think of all the clients he had that I could meet. We started with small talk and I presented my idea about how his clients could save on their insurance premiums with a discount of up to 20% for installing a security system. "I am well aware of that," he said and we continued to talk. About an hour and twenty minutes later, we knew each other's life stories. When I left, I had an appointment to meet him at his home the next morning to survey it for a system.

After we met and I quoted him a price, he then asked, if I would discount the system if I did his office as well. My heart started to pound. Wow, two sales in one meeting; this business is getting better. "I don't see why not," I replied. System two and three were about to be installed. Another $1400 profit, wow I'm on a roll!

The tree was starting to blossom.

The important thing was that I was starting to build a base for my recurring revenue I was now grossing $60 a month for the three systems I installed. Not bad for three weeks in business.

I didn't sell another system for almost two weeks. Charlie called me and said "I have a friend and client that is renovating a home in Tuxedo Park, and I told him about you. He would like you to call him and set up an appointment." "Thank you, I'll call him this afternoon."

I drove up to meet the prospective client on Saturday morning. Tuxedo Park is an exclusive private community of about 350 homes, located on 2,300 acres. The homes range in value from one to four million dollars. It is a gated community with its own private police force. It is also where the Tuxedo got its name from at the turn of the century.

I met Len Silverman at his nine-bedroom, 8,000 square foot, 80 year old mansion. The house was located on four acres of property. It bordered the park's 290 acre spring fed lake, which was over 100 feet deep in some places. Not only was the lake used for recreational activities, it was also used as the reservoir to supply drinking water to the community.

When I arrived, Len was in the backyard cleaning the leaves from his Olympic size swimming pool, which was about 50 feet to the right of his tennis court. Located behind the tennis court was a two bedroom guest cottage. It was late September, the weather was cooling and the leaves had begun to turn magnificent shades of red and gold.

"How do you do," I asked. "Glad to meet you," he replied. "Charlie spoke very highly of you. Why don't you come inside and look at the house?" We walked about 120 feet from the front end of his pool and entered the house through a rear door that led into a 9 by 13 foot pantry.

After touring the house, I felt overwhelmed that this job was so huge and would probably take me a week just to wire it. I figured the price and realized that if I closed the sale that there would be about $2000 in it for me. I really wanted this one. When I gave him the price, Len said, "Okay when can you install it?" I felt excited like my first trip to an amusement park. I was just handed a book of tickets and I could go on any ride I wanted to.

"Not for two weeks. I'm tied up until then," I replied. I didn't want him to think I didn't have any work to do. After all, if I wasn't busy how could I be that good?

It's a statement I use today when closing a sale and people tell me one of my competitors can install it right away. (Only now it is not just a line, we are normally so busy that three weeks is the norm, not an exception.) I usually answer, "Everyone in this business is so busy that they can't keep up with the work. Most of us work on referrals. If you don't get referrals, you don't work; except for the major national companies, none of us advertise. So if you are not that busy, how could you be that good?

If a painting contractor was giving you a proposal and said I'll be back in an hour what color do you want, you would probably wonder why he wasn't busy and would not hire him."

Two weeks later I installed Len's system, it took me three days by myself. My net profit on the job was almost $2,100. I felt a little guilty about making that much profit on the installation. After all, if you did the math I earned $700 a day, which was about what I used to gross in a week.

I found out later that he had two other proposals that were almost 40% higher than mine. I stopped feeling guilty.

CHAPTER 9
MY NICHE

Sometime in November, 1984, I stopped at a construction site to cold call the builder. I met George Starvos who was building a small subdivision of ten homes.

I had an idea how to include security systems in new construction at almost no cost to the new homeowner. If I installed a system in a new home and the buyer put the cost of the system into their mortgage, the difference in the payment to the bank each month would be offset by the amount they saved on their homeowner's insurance premium.

Also, I guaranteed that the system would be finished and operational before the closing, so that the builder could use it to protect the home against vandalism.

The problem at that time was that security systems were still a negative selling point. If the house came with a security system, many people wondered if the neighborhood was bad. So, I had to convince builders and real estate brokers that security systems were no longer negative.

My speech was simple; "Every system we install contains fire protection and panic buttons for police, fire and medical emergencies. The burglary part of a system is the least important. Burglars are sneak thieves that don't want to be in your home when you are there. It is a crime against your property, not you. I am more interested in the things that could get you hurt. Fire has no morality, it doesn't care if you are home or not, and it can start at any time. You can never be prepared enough for a medical emergency and if someone were to try to enter your home while you were there, your panic buttons would be working 24 hours a day. Also, all of our systems have an ambush or duress feature which works this way. If someone were to follow you into your home and force you to turn off your security system, you can disarm it with an alternate code, which not only turns off the system, but alerts the police at the same time."

George was a short Greek man about 50, with gray curly hair. I met him on the job site and tried to sell him my concept. It took about five meetings for me to convince him. I don't know if it was my persistence or if it was the coffee and rolls that I brought him every time we met.

My final meeting with him when I was about to close the deal sounded like this. "George you are building ten homes. Let me wire all of your homes as standard equipment. Don't pay me for the model, but let me use it as a showroom; this way you will save ten percent." "No," he said, "you do the model and I'll pay you, come up to Monroe and do my house." "What time do you want me there," I replied.

The first house I wired for him took me almost four days to complete. Today it takes us less that one day; of course I have two men on the job. It was in the middle of February and the bitter cold weather didn't help any. I silently prayed that all my wiring was correct and would stay intact, with all of the additional work that had to be done to complete the house. I worried about the sheet rockers cutting a wire by accident or the plumbers burning one when they soldered their heating pipes. As it turned out, when it came time to finish the system everything worked as it should. After I tested the system, I let out a sigh of relief that could have been heard in California.

Little did I know how this original chance meeting was going to make my business take off.

About a month later, George invited me to attend a Builder's Association meeting. He said that is where it all happens. I'll get to meet anyone and everyone from associate members such as real estate brokers, mortgage brokers, insurance brokers and at least 30 builders and remodelers. What a place to network.

My initial meeting was enough to convince me that this was the place to be. There were no other alarm installation companies that were members. I had the place all to myself.

I felt like I was first in line to buy World Series tickets. This was the fertilizer my trees needed. I believed I found my niche.

I have been a member now for over 18 years and to date there still are no other security companies that are members.

I started to network with everyone and anyone that was involved with home building and home sales. My big break came in the fall of 1985. I signed a contract which would enable us to be included on the options list for a townhouse development of 480 units.

My barrel started to fill.

Now it came time to hire some real help. A girlfriend of my oldest daughter was dating someone who was working for a security company as an installer. I met Robert during a party she was having at our house and asked him if he had time to work for me on the weekends to give me a hand.

He said, "Sure, I could use the extra money." We struck a deal and he started working for me every Saturday until I hired him full time three months later.

Six months into the project, the builder needed an incentive to help sell the units. Security systems were no longer an option, they became standard equipment. I felt like I just caught the winning touchdown pass in the Super Bowl. Along with the kitchen sink, you got a security system.

I bought another barrel.

CHAPTER 10
FINDING HEROES

I was sitting at my desk one morning when the phone rang. The voice on the other end of the line said, " H-H-H-Hi, m-m-my name is J-J-J-Joe C-C-C-Collis. A-a-a-are you hiring in-in-in-installers?" He was stuttering and stammering and I was having trouble understanding him. I said, "Speak slower and tell me why you are calling." I really thought someone was playing a joke on me.

Still stuttering, he was able to tell me that he just got laid off from his job that morning and picked up the yellow pages to call every company that was listed to see if they were hiring. I was impressed by his perseverance in trying to find a job immediately.

Joe went on to say, "I'm a g-g-g-reat technician, let me w-w-w-ork for you for a week for nothing and if I can't do the work you d-d-d-don't have to hire me." "No," I said, "if you work for me one hour you get paid, if it doesn't work out we part friends." "Where is your office," he inquired. "The office is in Spring Valley, New York. Where do you live?" "In N-N-N-Newburgh," was his answer. "You are about 35 miles north of me. I would like to meet you. I have to be in your area tomorrow to look at a job. How about meeting me about 9:00 A.M. and we can talk over coffee. Do you know where the Five Corners Diner is?" I asked. " Y-Y-Y-Yes." "Good I'll see you at nine." I was thinking about hiring another installer, but I thought to myself who needs someone who can't put a sentence together without stepping on his tongue. "By the way where did you work?" "H-H-H-Hammock Alarms." "I know the company you worked for," I said. "G-G-G-Good they can t-t-t-ell you a-a-a-about me." "Okay, I'll see you tomorrow."

I knew the owner of the company. I had met Max Hammock at a trade show about three months earlier and still had his business card in my rolodex. His company was located in Ulster County about sixty miles north of me, so we really weren't direct competitors.

I called Max and quickly reminded him where we had met. After exchanging the usual niceties, he explained to me that the only reason Joe was laid off is that things got slow and he was the last one hired. "I wanted to keep him over some of my other guys, but he was only with me about eight months and he is single. My other three people are married with families and have been with me at least four years. We had a big spurt in new installs for a large project we were doing. Things slowed down. I was hoping they would pick up but they didn't. You're going to like Joe. He is conscientious, trustworthy, a fast learner, never late for work and I don't remember him even being out sick for a day. It was a tough decision, but it came down to economics."

"What about his speech impediment?" I asked. "He's fine until he gets excited. His brain seems to run ahead of his mouth. If you get him to calm down you can understand him. He's a great worker and I'm sorry we had to let him go." "Thanks Max, I'm meeting with him tomorrow." "You won't be disappointed. Good luck," he added.

We met at the diner the next morning. Joe told me his life story and I told him mine. The meeting lasted about forty minutes and when it was over, I agreed to hire him for a two week trial period and if he worked out he would have a job.

Monday morning he met me on the job we were installing. The minute he picked up his tools, I knew I had a winner on my hands. His work habits and ethics were so outstanding that when he decided to move to California nine years later he gave me a one year notice.

I never thought I could replace him. But as I learned time and time again nobody's irreplaceable.

At this time I had four installers, Joe, Robert, Ronnie and Stan. I had a fifth installer that worked for me per diem. Danny was a sub-contractor that would hire himself out on a daily basis for the alarm industry. I was so busy that he would sometimes work for me two weeks at a time. I tried to hire him full time, but he was never interested. Danny would tell me that he liked his independence and didn't want to be tied down to a full time position.

I was in the office one morning when Danny called me to say he would need to take off for about a week. His father died suddenly of a massive heart attack. When he returned to work about ten days later, he approached me and explained that his 20 year old brother Dave, who worked with his dad in his automotive shop, needed a job. Danny said, "He's a fast learner, good with his hands and would probably work out great. Besides which, I really want to go into my own business someday and grow some equity. This way as long as I am here I can train him," he said. "Sure, have him call me, I'll talk to him. We could use another installer."

When I met Dave a few days later, all I saw as he came through the office door was his ponytail and tattoos. How can I put this guy in million dollar homes installing security systems, I thought. But, it didn't matter as we were doing so much new construction that the homeowners would never see him. After speaking with him for about twenty minutes, I decided to give him a try. Some of my Dad's lessons were kicking in. There are no rotten apples; they are just transportation vehicles for seeds. After all, I learned not to judge a book by its cover with Joe.

Was I pleasantly surprised?   Dave has been with me ten years. And if I thought Joe was a dynamo, Dave runs rings around him. He is neat, polite and my clients are always complimenting me on my installation staff. By the way, the ponytail is gone, Dave is now married with twins, and his television watching consists of the learning and history channels. His work ethics, skills and loyalty would make any employer glad to have him on their payroll. I'm sure Dave's dad would have been proud of him.

One of my dad's lessons to me was that no matter what you do in life, be the best you can. "If you want to be a ditchdigger, be the best damn ditchdigger there is," he would say.

My employees became my heroes.

CHAPTER 11

This chapter intentionally left blank.

CHAPTER 12
PLAY BALL

There is a joke about the last two words of the Star Spangled Banner being "Play Ball". My employees worked like they were a fine tuned baseball team.

If you were looking for the headquarters of the Mutual Admiration Society all you had to do was call my office. Ours wasn't an organized group; it just happened. If there was an organized society, its headquarters should have been in my office. I treated my employees with respect, I expected the same in return and I received it. The respect we had for each other was off the charts.

One of the things that I have always said is that I would never treat an employee the way I was treated when I worked in corporate environment after my time with Air Balance. Employees are people first. They have lives outside of the work place, which whether or not you want to believe it are sometimes more important than coming to work. If a family emergency would arise, I never wanted anyone to feel that if they didn't show up he or she would be judged poorly for taking time off. This was something that I imparted on them all of the time. "There is life outside of this company," I would say. I was paid back in spades. They would go an extra mile for me if needed. It was easy to see why; I treated them as people first and employees second. It also took the anxiety out of them the next time they called in with a problem. The last thing you want is anxious employees. They don't make happy workers.

There was also a business reason. If an employee called and said they were feeling sick, but would come in if I really needed them, my answer was always, "Stay home and rest up." I did not want them to come in, work outdoors, (especially in the winter) and get sicker; nor did I want them to infect anyone else. I would rather have an employee be out for one or two days of work than chance getting worse and being out for a week. If they infected a fellow worker I could have two people out for a week.

Nobody is indispensable. If you lose an employee for a day or two your business will not fall apart. If it does than you don't belong in business in the first place. When a senior executive or CEO of a major corporation suddenly dies, resigns or is dismissed nothing changes. It is business as usual. You just pick up the pieces and put them back together. Even when President John Kennedy was assassinated and President Richard Nixon left office nothing changed. The country didn't fall apart. We swore in a new leader and went on with our lives. It is no different in business.

People also need to be stroked. Everyone wants to be acknowledged and told that they did a good job. Even children need it, when your child cleans up their room, eats all of their dinner or gets a good grade on a test in school, they must be complimented. Employees are no different and there are many ways to acknowledge them.

I would always compliment them on a job well done when we finished an installation.

If a difficult installation was completed in less time than I allotted, I would sometimes give them a bonus for finishing early. If it was going the other way and it didn't look like we would finish on time, instead of them breaking for lunch I would buy lunch, deliver it to the job site, strap on a tool belt and help them finish. They appreciated it and I knew it.

Their compensation was more than any other technician in the industry doing the same work. They were worth it. We worked from 8:00 AM until 4:30 PM with a half of an hour break for lunch. If they finished an installation at 3:00 they went home early, but were paid for the rest of the day. If it went longer and they finished at 5:30 they were paid overtime. I wasn't losing on the installation.

A day's labor was figured into the price and if my technicians could finish it sooner, great!

I let my employees take home the company vehicles. There was a two fold reason for this. The first was that they didn't have any commutation expense which became part of their compensation if you figure in the savings to them. It was a nice perk. The second was a bonus to me.

Instead of having my technicians come to the office in the morning they would go directly to the client's house. If they started their day from the office, by the time they left and got to the job site, we would lose about 30 to 45 minutes. Having them show up on the job meant the installation was started at 8:00 AM instead of 8:45. If you do the math and take an average of two and one half hours a week per man times three men that equals more than 50 days a year in labor. Was it worth it to let them take the trucks home? You bet it was.

I would give my employees generous holiday bonuses. Most companies distribute them on or just before Christmas Eve. I always rewarded my employees at Thanksgiving. By receiving a bonus a month early they have plenty of time to shop and they didn't have to wonder or guess what their bonus would be while putting themselves in debt by charging everything on their credit cards. If they shopped early, had time on their hands just before the holidays and I needed them to work overtime, it was not a problem. They didn't say no because they had to go shopping.

We didn't have a holiday party before the holidays I would hold a dinner party after the New Year. I would invite all of my employees with their spouses or significant others to dinner at an expensive restaurant. My reasons for this were simple. During the holiday season it could be difficult for them to get a baby sitter; after all they want to go shopping too. I didn't want anyone to miss the celebration. It sometimes was difficult to find a restaurant to accommodate a large party during the holidays. But, the real reason was that having a celebration after the New Year seemed to extend the holidays. The impression of extending the holiday season kept my employees in a joyous mood.

Because they were happy as individuals, they became happy together. During an installation they worked like a well trained team. They worked well with each other and were always polite to each other. If someone needed help with a difficult task they would ask for it and it was gladly given.

They would explain to the homeowner why they were doing certain things in a particular manner. This many times relieved the anxiety of a homeowner who would be watching three or four technicians take apart their house. Would it ever be the same they wondered? Of course it was. I was told time and time again by my clients how well my technicians worked with each other. They sometimes had a cute sense of humor. On many occasions, at the end of the day after completing an installation, they would High-Five each other in front of the homeowner and say, "Not bad for our first job." The client hopefully knew they were kidding. I got the impression that they acted like a sports team that had just won an important game. It was really nice to see. I was proud of them. We worked like a team only I was the manager, coach, captain and team owner. We are all here for the good of the company. The better the company does, the better we all do.

I was friendly with my employees; I knew their wives and children. I would always ask how their families were doing; it was just my nature and not something I did consciously.

One of my dad's lessons was, "If you show people you care about them they will care for you in return." Dad was right.

CHAPTER 13
LIFE IS LIKE A RESEARCH PAPER

One of the many things my dad taught me was never say no to any opportunity. Put it on hold for a while, even if only for a few minutes, analyze what is needed or how the situation can best be handled or serve your interest.

He also said, "You don't have to know everything. Be a resource person. If you are unsure of how to handle a project or find yourself in a situation that is over your head, remember there is always someone out there that can help you out." Treat life like a research paper. Go to the library and look up the answers, he would say.

His example of this was the U.S. Presidency. Presidents don't get elected because they know everything. They get elected because they have bright ideas and know how to hire the right people to get the job done. It is the same in life. When you get a homework assignment in school you are not expected to know everything. That is why you are given textbooks; you are allowed to look up the answers.

So with this in mind, when a client of mine, Ray Mann, who owns an automotive body shop, called one day and asked me if we install Closed Circuit Television Cameras, I asked him what he needed.

I had never installed a C.C.T.V. system before and didn't know where to begin, but remembering my dad's teachings I didn't say no.

I met with him at his place of business and determined what he wanted to accomplish.

Ray needed to watch his parking lot where he stored customers' cars overnight. He had had a lot of vandalism recently and he wanted to not only prevent it, but hopefully catch the person or people responsible. I carefully took notes listing what his needs were. I told him I would get back to him in a few days.

When I returned to my office, I placed a telephone call to my distributor and asked him what he knew about C.C.T.V. His answer was swift and precise, "Call Bill Michaels from Surveillance

International. He is a manufacturer's rep and will also layout the job for you."

I thanked him and immediately called Bill. When he got on the telephone, I introduced myself and said, "Mark from King Distributors suggested I call you, this is what I need." I explained the situation. Bill said not a problem he would be happy to meet me on the job. "I do this all the time, its part of what I do," he said.

Two days later, Bill met me in my office. He gave me a loose-leaf binder containing brochures for all the products he sells. After talking for a few minutes over a cup of coffee, we drove over to Ray's shop. I introduced Bill to Ray as my C.C.T.V. Rep. He said, "Take a look around. If you need anything I'll be in the shop."

We surveyed the area and Bill made a sketch of the building and surrounding area. "I've got all I need. I can lay this out for you in about an hour. Let's head back to your office," he said. We said goodbye to Ray and I told him I would get back to him that afternoon.

In my office, Bill worked up a list of what equipment I would need and what my cost would be. He drew a quick pencil sketch of how to wire the cameras and listed what type of wire I would need. "All of the parts are in stock, so there is no problem with delivery," he added.

I had my equipment costs, all I needed to do now was add my labor, overhead and profit margin and I was ready to talk to Ray.

I called Ray and presented my proposal to him. "Here is what you will need. Three low light cameras in weather resistant housings, two stationary cameras for the front of the building and one pan unit to view the entire side yard on the north end of your shop. You will also need a 17 inch monitor, a Multi-Plex unit to split the images on the monitor and a Time Lapse Video Recorder that will record on a standard VHS tape for up to 72 hours. Your total cost would be $11,300.

"Is this a lease or do I own it?" he asked. "You own it," I replied. "Can I lease it?" I did not provide leasing, but I was certain I could find someone to finance it. "I have my own leasing company. Would you work with them," Ray asked. "That's no problem at all." "I'll get back to you in a few days. In the meantime, fax me the proposal." "Consider it done," I replied.

Ray put together the financing and we installed the system two weeks later. Bill was also there. After we connected all the equipment, he helped to fine tune any of the equipment that needed adjusting.

Since that time we have installed over 120 C.C.T.V. systems.

So I learned to analyze every situation before I say no. Many people in and out of business have a fear about trying something new. If you don't explore your options, you will not expand your horizons and grow. As dad said, "You have to stick your hand in that barrel. If you don't like what you come up with, you can always put it back."

As I was writing this chapter I was reminded of a situation that came to my attention when I was working at Air Balance. John Marino, who was our export manager, came into my office with an inquiry from the Royal Canadian Air Force. They were interested in two fire control dampers that would be installed in a military bunker. They had to withstand the force of a direct hit of a one megaton bomb. John asked, "How on earth do you seismically test them? Are they crazy," he added.

I thought for a moment, then said sign off on it, add 50% for the certification and write them a letter that we can fulfill their needs.

"You're as crazy as they are," he added. "No I'm not. If the building takes a hit, the dampers are inside. As long as the building is there, the dampers will be there. What's the downside, we refund their money.

So the simple lesson my dad passed along to me has worked for me many times. Stop, think and analyze the situation. You may be surprised at the outcome.

CHAPTER 14
STAYING IN TOUCH

B y the time I completed my second year in business, I was working for four builders who were planning to construct over 600 homes and condominiums over the next four years and a building boom in housing was in the making. By 1989, we had completed over 900 homes.

Today I am working for 27 builders and have completed over 2,800 homes under construction. New construction accounts for over 70 % of our annual installations. The balance of my clients comes from referrals. My advertising budget is the smallest part of my overhead. Except for my yellow page ad and my web site, I do not advertise.

From the time I started Pro-Tech Security, to date, I have grown the company at a steady rate of over 20% a year.

I have eight employees, six installation and service technicians and two in administrative help.

Currently we are doing over 1.4 million dollars in sales annually, of which over 50% is from recurring revenue.

Pro-Tech Security is also the only company in the area that offers service contracts on the equipment we install. It is amazing that the average person doesn't want to touch any appliance if it breaks. All they want to do is make a phone call and have someone come over and fix it utilizing a service contract, which is no more than an insurance policy. Security systems are no exception.

Customer service is the most important part of my business. When someone calls for service and asks when we can send someone to their home, our response is, "When are you home next?" If for example, the response is that they get home from work at 5:30, our answer is, "We will have someone at your home by 6:00."

One of the reasons we have been so successful is that we service our clients at their convenience, not ours. We will service them at 7:00 A.M., before they leave for work or at 6:00 P.M. when they return. Weekends are no exception to this rule.

People are so familiar to the response they receive from telephone or appliance repair companies telling them that someone will be at their home next Tuesday between noon and five P.M. This usually means someone has to be home to let them in, if they show up at all.

We give our customers a thirty minute window. Usually we arrive on time, if not, we call and tell them exactly what time to expect us. The difference is, we show up. If we miss a service appointment, and we have missed very few, when we return there is no charge for the service call.

With about 4,200 systems installed, we have only about seven to ten service appointments a week. The reason for this is that we install our systems with such care that there are very few problems to correct. Most of our service calls involve homeowners changing windows or doors that have to be rewired. That is why service contracts can be so profitable. If you install it correctly the first time, you rarely have to go out and make a repair. You can send them a bill once a year for not fixing it. Is that an oxymoron or what? But when something does go wrong, the customer has peace of mind knowing that the repair is covered under the contract.

Customer contact is extremely important to me. You must stay in touch with your customers. You want to be in up front in their minds at all times. We are the only company in the metropolitan area that publishes a four-color newsletter, which is titled, *"The Monitor."*

Each edition contains articles dealing with security issues, such as how to make sure your home looks occupied when you are away, to identity theft, which includes the telephone numbers and web sites of all the credit reporting fraud bureaus. I also write articles on false alarm prevention to help reduce unnecessary police response. The newsletter is used to sell additional products and services. The front page always contains a personal message from me, which continually thanks our clients for their continued trust and confidence in us.

In 2003, a national trade magazine chose the *Monitor* as one of the best newsletters in the industry.

My newsletter is a tool I use when making a sales call. I leave at least two back issues with all of the other literature I use during my presentation with the prospective client. It starts with a presentation folder I purchased from a national mail-order printing company. The folder is heavy stock paper with my company name printed on the front. The second line contains the message "*a life safety company*" and the third line is our telephone number and web site address.

I prepare the folder with about eight pieces of literature in it, which I obtain free from my vendors and manufacturers. Included as well is a list of insurance companies and what their discounts are for people who have security systems, copies of my newsletter and an introductory letter that explains the company mission, which is "to protect life and property." By the time I get finished, the package is so informative and heavy that it takes over two dollars in postage to mail it. It makes me look more professional than any of my competitors and I have been told, time and time again, that I was awarded the job because of my professionalism.

CHAPTER 15
WHAT TO DO WITH ALL THESE APPLES

B y the end of 1988, we were extremely profitable. It wasn't that we were charging exorbitant prices; it was that I was buying my products better. Reducing my cost of goods sold is the easiest way to increase profits without raising prices.

One thing I did was to contact a local wire manufacturer that I knew. I stopped in to see the owner of the company to inquire what he does with his mill ends that he cannot sell. I was buying our wire on one thousand foot spools and knew that he had to have odd lots that were on the end of a run. Most of these rolls were between 800 and 990 feet long.

"What happens to the ends of your master rolls after you boxed all of your wire," I asked the owner of the company. "We have a warehouse full of it out back," was his response. "How much would you sell it to me for if I take it off your hands?" "What are you paying now?" "Thirty-one dollars a thousand," I replied. "How about sixteen dollars a thousand?" "How much do you have there?" I countered. "I'm not sure; it has to be at least a half a million feet." "I'll take every roll you have that has a minimum of four hundred feet. I will pay you fourteen dollars, pick it up and have it out of your warehouse within a week." "That's a deal," he replied.

As it turned out, there wasn't a single roll that was less than 800 feet. I had enough wire to last almost a year and a half. I knew how busy we were going to be over the next two years, so stock-piling wire was no problem. I saved over $8,500 in material costs that went right to the bottom line.

One of my technicians asked me, what we were going to do with all that wire.

I said, "It's like having too much gas in your car; it's not going to go to waste, eventually you are going to use it."

I was reading the Sunday New York Times Business Section one day. I noticed an advertisement for the auction of a hardware store that had gone bankrupt. I attended the auction and purchased all the screws, drill bits, and miscellaneous hardware that we could use, for pennies on the dollar.

My theory was, try to keep your prices in line by buying your raw materials better, but never sacrifice quality.

I was saving so much money on the purchasing side of my business that naturally my gross profit margins began to grow rapidly. My profits were so high that it was almost embarrassing.

I called my accountant and asked him what I should do with all of the additional money we were earning. He said jokingly, "You can donate it to your friendly accountant's entertainment fund."

"What if I were to set up a charitable foundation?" I asked. "It would probably take as much time and effort to run a foundation than it does to run your business."

"What if I just donated it to a local charity?" "You can do that, but you won't get the tax deduction, remember you are a Sub Chapter S Corporation," he stated.

"Okay, let me think about it," I said.

After some self brainstorming, I devised a plan that would allow me to get the tax break, without actually taking the deduction.

I decided to pick a charity to donate to. I would allow my clients to reduce the cost of their installation if they would write a check to the charity and this way they would get the deduction. It was a win-win for all concerned.

I wanted to give back to the community we were servicing, so I chose a local fund that was called the "Tomorrows Children's Fund". I picked this organization because of a client of mine who had lost a teenage son to cancer and was actively involved with the organization. They were building an addition onto a local hospital in his name and needed financial help.

What I did was reduce every new installation invoice by $50, if the client would write a second check payable to the fund.

The next time I renewed my yellow pages advertisement, I included in my ad that you will receive a tax deduction with every new system we install. Within days of the new telephone book being distributed, some of my competitors called, disguising their voices or having someone call for them, trying to find out what the deduction was. We wouldn't tell them.

Not only did I have my competitors baffled; it also increased the calls we were getting from the telephone book. This in turn led to more business which increased the charitable contributions.

I was involved with the "Tomorrows Children's Fund" for about three years. At the same time, I was also actively involved with the Builder's Association creating a local fund called "Community Outreach". Through this fund we would build wheelchair ramps, widen doorways, and do anything else that was necessary to make physically challenged children's lives easier. I would donate an additional $25 for every system I installed in a newly constructed home.

After the outpatient center at the hospital was completed, I became involved with a local community based organization known as "Camp Venture". The Venture organization is a not for profit agency providing services to people with mental retardation and developmental disabilities. They are spread out in many residential settings throughout the community and have a large new rehabilitation facility. They were trying to raise money to build a swimming pool. Once again, I gave up a portion of our sales. When their new facility and pool was dedicated two years later, I was surprised and flattered to find a plaque on the wall that read, "This pool was made possible through the generous support of Pro-Tech Security."

In 1995, I became aware that our local Meals on Wheels offices were burglarized. I called the director, whom I knew, and told her that my technicians were going to be at her offices to install a security system the next morning at no cost to them.

She was extremely grateful. Little did I know that this little act of kindness on my part was going to be the beginning of my involvement with the organization for years to come.

Over the years my involvement with Meals on Wheels has led to my being asked to join the Board of Directors. It has enabled me to help raise hundreds of thousands of dollars for them. I am still a member of the board today.

In October of 2003, at a fund raising dinner, I was honored as Humanitarian of the Year. I was also honored by the New York State Senate and Assembly in a resolution commending my accomplishments.

My dad's lesson about filling that barrel and leaving some for the other guy was really working. I had more than I could use, so why not give them away.

CHAPTER 16
GO FLY A KITE

I built my business on my strengths, not my competitors' weaknesses. Learning what not to do, as much as what to do has contributed to my success. I learned to stay more than one step ahead of not only my immediate competitors, but the major public companies in my business that were trying to buy up all the small businesses in my field.

This recently has taken place in the funeral home industry in the United States. The only difference between the security industry and the funeral industry is that in the funeral home industry they allow the owner to keep running their business on a salary or commission, thereby keeping the name and business reputation intact.

In the security alarm industry, a major company will buy your existing accounts, immediately change your customers over to their service and bill them under their name. Most small companies such as mine that are billing out over one million dollars annually have been built on a small local reputation such as the local funeral home. So why not keep the company running with the existing owner, pay them a commission, increase the account base and run it as a wholly owned subsidiary?

The large competitors are usually one of the national companies that advertise on radio and television with a low-ball price. People are leery about doing business with them. Most of my clients have been told by me that these companies are scam artists who don't care about your security; they just want to get that monthly service fee.

I have found that those national companies that buy up small companies lose about 15% to 20% of the accounts within three to six months. This is usually due to the fact that the small dealer has very weak contracts with their subscribers. I have seen many of their contracts; for the most part they do not have an assignment clause.

I have purchased seven small companies since I have been in business. My requirement is that the selling dealer has all of his clients sign my contract. I want a guarantee that they are now my clients. We send a letter to all of them explaining that, in order to service you better LMNOP Alarm Co. and Pro-Tech Security

Systems are merging. Your service will remain the same. I also require the seller to be available for service even if by telephone for one year after the closing. I hold back 10% in escrow for that year to insure their compliance. To date, I have never lost a client account that I have purchased.

The national companies usually send an invoice when it is due with a note that your contract has been purchased and this is what your new bill is going to look like. Take it or leave it.

One local company in my area, sold out to another medium-sized company, which then sold to a larger company who then sold to a national public company, one of the largest in the U.S. All of this happened within two years. Clients of the original company had no idea who they were doing business with anymore and didn't know who to call for service.

After the third sale, we took over the service of 23 customers of the original company; not by soliciting them, but by them calling us for help with their systems. I can only imagine how many other clients my competitors picked up.

It is like flying a kite. If you have more string than the next guy you can fly your kite higher than anyone else, only the winds are so strong up high that you lose control of your kite. It's no different in business. Stretch yourself too far, too fast and you will lose control.

I have been able to beat the major competitors in the industry at their game by exposing their scams during my sales presentation. When a potential client asks me why I charge for installations when they can get it for free from a major competitor, I show them my competitor's contract which says that the equipment remains the property of the seller and if the customer were to cancel their monitoring agreement the company may remove all of the equipment and collect the balance of the monitoring contract. Some companies sell the contract to a finance company and get all of their money up front. It is nothing more than a no money down lease.

What happens if you sell your home and the equipment is removed? The homebuyer during the final walk through wants to know what happened to the security system that was in the home when he first went to contract with you. Well, guess what you are going to have to come up with at the closing? That's right, about $1,500 for the missing system. Besides the free or cheap system is not a complete system, it only protects two doors and includes a motion detector, one keypad and siren. It does not include fire protection or any other window or door protection. Yes, they will sell you all the additional protection you really need, usually at full price, which is almost twice as expensive as a system we can install, but you still may not own it. I describe this in a marketing piece that I wrote called the *"Free Alarm"*. I compare it to an HMO, it reads as follows:

"Want a free alarm? Don't bet your life on it because that is just what you might be doing. Why would you think someone is going to give you something for free? Do you really believe that a company would give away their products and continue to stay in business? Did the word free get your attention? Would you accept free medical insurance if it only covered you for colds and sore throats?

Well, here is how it works. The so called 'free state of the art security system' you hear advertised is no more then a lease disguised as a free system. What they are going to do is protect two doors and install a motion detector in your home and only if you sign a long-term monthly contract for about twice the price we would charge. What they don't tell you is that they will sell off your contract to a finance company. You have little protection and they get all their money up front.

What happens if a burglar comes in through an unprotected basement window while you are sleeping? What if you have a fire with no fire protection included with your system?

At Pro-Tech Security, we will only install a system as though it is our home. I have to leave your home after the installation and know that it is protected in such a way that I would allow my family to sleep there.

If you want a free system, don't call us. However, if you want to be protected from more than colds and sore throats our number is 845-555-1234. "

At a home improvements show I was exhibiting at, a major security alarm company was also selling their systems. The company was a multi-million dollar public corporation. A young couple came up to me. The husband handed me a contract he had just signed with the major competitor and asked me if I could beat the price.

I asked him if he knew that it is a lease and that he will be paying back more money than the system was worth and that he was getting no protection at all. He said no. They told him that they were going to install the system in his home for $149.00. I turned over the contract and asked him to read two paragraphs. The first said that the title to the system remained with the competitor and that if they cancelled their service the company can remove all the equipment, and that the customer will have to pay off the balance of the contract. The second said that they have the right to assign this contract without notifying the buyer.

I said that if he wanted to, I could come to his home and design a system that would be right for his family and he could decide if he still wanted to install theirs or mine.

His reaction to what he just read was very straight forward. He said to his wife, "This is a rip off." He gave me his name and telephone number, asked me to call him and left to cancel the agreement he had signed.

About a week later I received a letter in the mail from the salesperson's manager on corporate stationery stating that I caused them to lose a sale, was guilty of slandering his company and if I didn't stop it immediately they were going to proceed with legal action against me.

I called his office and spoke to his district manager. I read him the letter I had just received and told him that a threat of that nature could be a crime and that if he didn't want a lawsuit for malicious threats, he'd better do something about it. I faxed him a copy of the letter. The next day I received a telephone call from their legal department apologizing for the sales manager's actions. I said the apology was not good enough. "I want him gone, he is a disgrace to the industry," I said. "It's been done," was the reply, "we cannot have people on the payroll that put us in jeopardy like that." I guess I really had them greatly concerned.

Three days later the sales manager called me. He began his conversation with every four-letter word you can imagine and threatened to break my legs for getting him fired. As soon as I was able to get a word in the conversation, I informed him that all our calls were recorded for quality assurance and that if he didn't want to get arrested for telephone harassment he had better hang up now and never call again. "Click," I never heard from him again.

My marketing plan was not to advertise any specials; price is for the companies that believe that price is the only thing that people shop. Their belief is that the cheaper the price the easier it was to sell.

My dad's lessons of be the best you can be, no matter what you do, was really working. I sell quality not price.

CHAPTER 17
IT'S NEVER ON SALE

I believe that there is a clear distinction between marketing and selling, maybe it goes back to my earlier days with the printing company whose psychologist said I was like the Navy. You have got to get their attention first. My theory is that when marketing, you have to provide a need for the product then convince them that they really need your product and then close the sale.

The difference I perceive between marketing and a sale is simply to let them think you are the only game in town and put your name everywhere they can see it. Every place they turn, you want them to see your name. But never mention price. Make them want to do business with you because they want to be a member of your special club. I want to do business with you because you appear to be the biggest and the best. But you better back it up with deeds not just words.

Here is a perfect illustration of this. If you needed a muffler for your automobile where would you go? Does the name Midas ring a bell? Why? Not because they are the best and cheapest, but because you are familiar with the name. Why do you know the name? You see it all over the place, television, radio, newspapers, billboards, etc. Did you know that you could probably get a muffler from your local mechanic and maybe cheaper? Is there a big difference between the muffler you get from your local mechanic or Midas? Probably not, a muffler is a muffler. But Midas seems to be the biggest and best. They are good at what they do and they back up their products with service and integrity.

So why pick Midas, when you could go anywhere? Because you know the name, it has been rubber stamped in your brain; they are the only name you see day in and day out.

But you never hear them mention a sale or price.

So based on this theory, I wanted everyone to think of Pro-Tech Security when they thought of a system for their home or business.

I embarked on a campaign of getting Pro-Tech's name everywhere.

One of the first things I did was to order lawn signs for homes. When we installed a system I would install a sign on their mailbox post or within their landscaping that was about fifteen inches in diameter and was shaped like a police shield. It was red and white with black lettering that read Protected by Pro-Tech Security Systems. It included our telephone number on it.

They started to show up everywhere. When I would go out on a sales call, I would take one with me and show it to the potential client. The response many times was, "So you are that company I see everywhere, you must be the largest company in the county. I see your logo everywhere." Even my competitors were starting to take notice. But it took seven years before any of them offered lawn signs. The first one that did copied my logo exactly. I didn't have a copyright on the shield so I couldn't have an exclusive.

The only difference between his sign and mine was the name and color. He used the same colors but reversed the order of them. People would think that his signs were mine. At a quick glance, while you were driving, the signs looked the same. It was great. My competitors were helping to get my message out. It is amazing how you can get people to work for you and not include them on your payroll.

As time went by, I was so busy that keeping up with the work was getting frustrating. We were working six days a week for almost a year with no letup in sight. The problem was finding additional competent help. We were busier than any of my competitors, even the ones that were in business years longer then me.

I was starting to run out of barrels.

I was having lunch with one of my vendors that I did over $200,000 worth of business with on an annual basis. David Lang was the branch manager of the distribution center that serviced my account. He asked me, "What are you doing with all that equipment you are buying? None of your competitors order that much. Are you giving it away?" "No as a matter of fact we are at least 20% higher-priced than anyone else," I replied. "How can that be?" he asked. "It is very simple, people can have three things. They can have quality, service and price. If all they want is price and they want it cheap, they are not going to get quality and service. If they want to do business with me and want quality and service they have to pay the price."

"For example, I install a system in a home in one day; in by 8:30 A.M. and out by 4:30 P.M. Most of my competitors take three days to complete the same job. The reason why is that they lowball every job and never make enough money to hire and train. I charge a few dollars more because I have real overhead and they don't. When I first went into business, my profits were through the roof. I was a one man shop at the time with no overhead. That only lasted about six months.

Now it is different, I have a $350,000 payroll and 28% overhead on top of that. I would love to earn what I did on the first few systems I originally installed, but that's not about to happen. Most of my competitors are still a one or two man operation. They do not have any office help. When you call, you get an answering machine that tells you to leave a message or page them if it is an emergency. They usually work out of their home and many times have to leave a job in the middle to handle some emergency. Many times they don't even show up the next day.

The homeowner will take two or three days off from work to stay at home while the installation takes place. What's three days of vacation time worth these days? Why not pay about $250 to $300 more to have the job done in one day; no messy house for three days and no lost vacation or sick time. When we leave your home, it will be as spotless as it was when we arrived. Except for the new security equipment we installed you won't even know anyone worked there that day.

I have competed with the biggest and the best and I beat them at their games. I don't have any gimmicks only the honest truth."

"It's unbelievable, I remember when you first went into business," David said. "I have been in this business over forty years and I have never seen a company grow as fast as yours. Even your competitors have noticed, they seem to be jealous of what you are doing," he added. "I'm sorry to hear that," I replied. "I don't like anyone watching me; it's like an evil eye." "No, I mean that sincerely. It is a pleasure to do business with you. Besides the amount of equipment you buy from me, you know what you are doing better than anyone else I know in this business. I heard you were nominated for Security Dealer of the Year for the second time." "Yes, it is really an honor." "That's fantastic, you deserve it. It would be nice to have bragging rights as the best security company in America," he said.

"I'm just trudging along filling up barrels," I said. "What's that supposed to mean?" he asked. "Just something my dad taught me."

CHAPTER 18
SHORT SLEEVES

It has always amazed me how some of the largest companies stay in business. The levels of incompetence I have encountered are amazing.

The following story is absolutely true; it is so unbelievable that it could not be made up. I even have the paperwork to prove it.

One of the other things I did was have all of my employees wear uniform shirts that had the company logo on them. I ordered shirts from a well-known catalogue company. They were reasonably priced and would do the right job. My first order was for long sleeve denim blue shirts with our logo directly embroidered on it with the employees' name on the opposite breast. I ordered six shirts for each of my employees with their names on them and an additional two dozen without names to give away to some friends and a select few builders that we worked for. There were sixty shirts in all with a cost of about $30.00 each.

The shirts arrived about three weeks later; everything was just as I had ordered.

Sometime in February, I repeated the order with one variation. I wanted the exact same shirts only with short sleeves for the spring and summer months.

I placed the order and the company faxed me a confirmation.

About four weeks later, the shirts arrived and they were red instead of blue. I called their customer service department and was told that they would reorder them. The customer service representative apologized and said they would send me a United Parcel Service Call Tag to pick them up. She further stated that they would credit the invoice.

Sometime in the beginning of April, the replacement order arrived. When I opened the carton I found that the shirts were the right color, but instead of direct embroidery on the shirts, our company logo was on patches that were sewn onto the shirt.

"What's going on?" I asked the customer service representative. "Can't your people get it right? This is the second time these shirts were ordered. All I asked for is a reorder of the same shirts as before; the only difference is I want them in short sleeves." I'm sorry was the answer. "I will personally see to it that they are correct this time." Somehow, I didn't believe her. I also said, "The problem is the weather is changing, it is getting warmer out, and I need these shirts as soon as possible. Please see what you can do to rush this order." "I will have them for you within ten days," she promised.

Two weeks later three boxes of shirts arrived. I turned to my office manager and said "Any bets?" "You don't think they would screw it up a third time?" she asked. As I removed the first shirt from the box, she said, "It looks like they finally got it right." "No they didn't," I replied. "Look at the color of the embroidery; they reversed the colors. It's wrong again."

This time my call to them was not very polite. "So far you have managed to screw-up three orders in a row. Now you want me to give you a fourth chance? To make matters worse, you are sending me past due notices for the first two invoices, charging me interest for a past due account and ruining my credit rating. How are you going to make up for your incompetence?" I asked.

The person I was speaking to asked me to hold on for a minute. When she got back on the line she said, "Give us one more chance, we will give you a 20% discount and not charge you freight. I promise we will rush the order and have it to you in four days." "Okay," I said, "This is your last chance."

On the fifth day the order arrived. I sat down on the floor in the office and opened the first box. I began to laugh uncontrollably. I felt like a child being tickled, laughing so hard I couldn't catch my breath. What I was looking at was not funny. The shirt I held in my hand was a long sleeve sweatshirt with a printed logo on the back from a delivery service in Rhode Island.

I called the same customer service representative that I had been previously dealing with during this entire fiasco. When I told her what I had just received, there was a long silent pause on the telephone. "I don't know what to say," she said. "I do," I answered, "you will have these shirts out of my office within two days or I am throwing them in the garbage. You will credit my account for all past and future invoices and you will take me off your mailing list. I don't ever want to receive another catalogue from you again. Is that understood?" "Yes, Mr. Solomon." "Goodbye," I said.

The entire price of all the wrong orders totaled about $7,200. It took close to four months to straighten out all of the invoices and credits. I am only one customer, but I'm sure they must waste hundreds of thousands of dollars each year on others as well. How can they stay in business?

If you ever wanted a lesson in quality control this was it. It was apparent that someone in their company didn't do their job. All they had to do was check one order against the next and it would have come out right the first time.

I keep using other people's incompetence as fertilizer for my tree.

CHAPTER 19
THE HOOSIER STATE

A bout three years after we installed our first Closed Circuit Television System, I was ordering over $24,000 worth of equipment for another surveillance system. The cameras I needed for the installation were highly sophisticated and required military specifications. The manufacturer was Diamond Electronics, a division of a multi-national corporation, one of the oldest on the New York Stock Exchange. They sold the equipment I needed direct, which meant I didn't have to go through a distributor. I was assigned a salesperson named Sandy Browne. I told him what I needed and asked if it was possible to have the equipment within two weeks. Sandy said that wouldn't be a problem. As soon as I get your purchase order, I can ship it out immediately. "Will a fax get you started," I asked. "Yes, but also send me two copies of the original." "No problem," was my reply.

I faxed him my purchase order and mailed them two originals. It contained a list of all the equipment I was ordering along with a promised delivery date of on or before September 14th, which is what Sandy had promised me. The equipment was being shipped by truck from their warehouse in Pennsylvania. The purchase order's instructions were very clearly stated: bill to and ship to the same, Pro-Tech Security Systems, 2 Post Road, Monsey, N.Y. I also wrote a note on the purchase order for the driver to call for instructions if he couldn't find our office.

On September 14th, when it didn't arrive, I called Sandy to see if it had been shipped on time. "Your order left here on the sixth. It was packed in five cartons on two skids," was his answer. "That was eight days ago, you're only two days away. Was it consolidated?" I asked. "No it was shipped Roadway Express." "Then it should have been here. I need it by the end of the week. We are installing it on Monday." "I will put a trace on it," was his reply. "One of our expediters will call you as soon as they find out what happened."

The next morning I received a call from Roadway Express. I was told my order was delivered on the tenth and signed for by Ed Fisk. "I don't have anybody who works for me with that name," I replied. "Are you sure you have the right order?" "Yes, five cartons on two skids, going to Pro-Tech Security from Diamond Electronics, signed by Ed Fisk." "What is the shipping address it went to?" I asked. "Two Post Road, Muncie, Indiana," was the answer. (Somewhere in

Muncie, Indiana there is another Post Road in a commercial area.) *"INDIANA!"* I shouted into the phone. "What are you saying? That order is supposed to be in Monsey, New York; not Muncie, Indiana." "We only transported it. All the paperwork from the vendor says, 2 Post Rd., Muncie, Indiana. Take it up with the shipper."

I called Diamond. I was furious. I was told Sandy, the salesman who wrote the order, was at lunch. I asked for the shipping department. When a shipping department clerk answered the telephone, I immediately asked for a supervisor. Within one minute, a woman got on the line. I explained to her what I had found out. She said to hold on and she would pull the paperwork. When she got back on the line she said, "The order is correct, it was shipped to where you wanted it to go." "What are you talking about? My office is in New York not Indiana." "All of our paperwork says Muncie, Indiana." "How can that be? My purchase order instructed you to ship it to Monsey, New York." "But, I can only go by what our paperwork says." "I don't care what your paperwork says. My paperwork said Monsey, New York. Do you have a copy of my purchase order?" "I'll have to go to the file and look for it. I will call you back." "No you won't! I'll hold on. You have $24,000 of my equipment floating around somewhere in Indiana and I need it here by Friday, today is Wednesday." "Okay, hold on," she said.

When she returned about seven minutes later, she stated that the person who wrote up the order said she never heard of Monsey,

New York, but knew there was a Muncie, Indiana, so she shipped it there. "Who do you have working for you, idiots?" I asked. "How can she arbitrarily change a shipping address because she never heard of Monsey, New York? These are preprinted forms," I told her. "Do you think I have thousands of dollars of stationery printed up with a New York address just to confuse some shipping clerk? Now what do we do?" She said, that they will have to locate the order in Indiana and have it shipped back to their warehouse, then re-route it to me. "I guess you weren't listening to me. I need that order here within two days," I said. "How can I get you your equipment if it is in Indiana?" "You can't. What you do is duplicate the order, send it to me priority express and go find the equipment you sent to Muncie, Indiana. It's that simple." She said she didn't have the authority to do that. I asked her who did and she replied, she didn't know. "You have ten minutes to find out who does. While you are doing that connect me to the salesman who wrote the original order."

Sandy didn't answer his phone, so I left him a voicemail message explaining my order wound up across the country and to please call me immediately.

It was less than a half-hour later when Sandy called back. I filled him in on what had transpired during my last conversation with his shipping department. He sounded flabbergasted. "Let me call you back within twenty minutes," he said. "I will call you either way," he added.

The phone rang within ten minutes, it was him, "Here's what we are going to do," he said. "We are duplicating the order and shipping it this afternoon. The bad news is that we don't have the complete order in Pennsylvania. We have to ship it from our warehouse in Madison, Wisconsin. The earliest I can have it to you is Monday. We will pick up the freight cost," he added. "I guess I'll have to live with it," I countered. "Believe me, if we don't get that equipment back from Indiana, heads are going to roll."

I didn't want to belabor the point about the shipping clerk's screw up. So I just said, "Sandy, I guess it is hard to fly like an eagle when you are working with turkeys." He just laughed and we said goodbye.

Two things happened Monday; first it rained all day, second the order didn't arrive until late in the afternoon. The installation was outdoors so we had to postpone it until the weather changed.

My dad always said things have a funny way of working out, just when you least expect it.

CHAPTER 20
IT DOESN'T COMPUTE

I have found that trying to do business with large national firms is not easy.

In 1993, I had purchased a 24/7 parts and labor service contract from a nationally known computer manufacturer and distributor when we upgraded our computers. The contract was to insure that I could get in-house service for our file server and any workstation listed on the contract the next business day. The contract came complete with an 800 toll-free number to call for service. The contract cost about $900 for two years and included three workstations and our file server.

Early in the second year of the contract, one of our workstation's hard drives failed and was in need of immediate repair.

I called the 800 number for service only to be connected to an amazing series of telephone prompts to get to the party I was trying to reach. After about three minutes on the phone, I pressed "0" to try to get to an operator. The recorded message said that this was an unacceptable choice and returned me to the beginning of the menu.

After trying for about another five minutes, a real voice got on the line. I explained what I needed and was informed that I had the wrong department. "Please, can you connect me to someone who can help me," I replied. "Just a minute," was the answer. The next voice I heard was the same recording that I had just listened to for the last five minutes. I was so frustrated that if you could measure the anger I felt, I would have broken the meter. I just wanted to slam the phone down, but didn't. I don't know how, but I somehow was able to get to the right service department only to be told that they will take the information and someone from their local repair service office would call me to set up an appointment.

I asked where they were located and was told in White Plains, New York. White Plains is about twelve miles from my office. I asked, "Could I have the telephone number of that office?" "I'm sorry, but we are not allowed to give it out, they will call you within 72 hours." "That's three days," I said, "what about my twenty-four/seven contract?" "Oh, that only means you can call us twenty-four/seven; it doesn't mean we will fix it in twenty-four hours."

My frustration and anger was only getting more intense. I was at their mercy and there was nothing I could do about it.

The next day the service company called. They wanted to set up an appointment for two days later and said that they would be in the area sometime that morning between 9:30 and 12:00. I asked if they could possibly make it any sooner. "That's the best we could do," was the reply.

Two days later a service technician showed up and informed me that the hard drive in my workstation needed to be replaced. The machine would have to be taken to their office, the part had to be ordered and returned within ten days. I was ready to scream. "What about my twenty-four/seven contract," I asked. "Hey, I only fix them, I don't make the rules," he said.

They called two days later and informed me that they were able to locate the part needed and would return the computer the next day.

About four months after the machine was returned, the hard drive failed again. I was able to get service on it within one day (I guess they weren't busy and able to send someone out right away). When the technician opened up the workstation and removed the hard drive I was told, "This drive is not a factory original part and it is not covered under your contract." "That is the part your company put in last time; no one touched that computer but your technicians. I don't know what parts they put in, I only know that your company did it and as far as I'm concerned it is covered," I replied. "I'm sorry," he said, "I am only allowed to work on original factory installed parts under your service plan and this one doesn't comply."

"Get your boss on the phone," I said.

He called his office and told someone on the other end of the line what he found when he opened up the machine.

I said, "Let me talk to them. Hello, could you tell me what's going on with this computer?" I asked. "It's very simple," the person on the other end said, "you got a Ford with a Chevy engine in it."

"You're the guys that put the Chevy engine in, so I expect you to work on it," I replied. "You don't know that," he countered. "We are a factory authorized service center. Why would we put a generic hard drive in your computer?" "Someone else must have worked on it," he said. "If you want us to fix it, we can, but it will cost you about $600." "No one touched that workstation except your technician," I said. "That's what you say, I don't know that. If you want us to fix it, let me know, but your service contract is void because it doesn't contain original factory parts," he said. I was so angry. I felt as though my blood was about to boil. I hung up the telephone and turned to his technician.

"I would like you to leave my office," I said. That is when it almost got ugly. He said, "I need you to sign this service ticket and there will be a $135 charge for the service call." "I will sign nothing and don't even think of sending me a bill. I suggest you leave my office now before I have the police remove you. As far as I'm concerned, right now you are trespassing." The technician just turned and left. I never got an invoice or ever heard from them again.

The next day I ordered a new workstation that was more powerful than the one I replaced. It cost me about $1,400 and was in service for about five years without a single problem until we upgraded our entire network. We now have a new file server with three workstations that give us little or no problem at all.

The contracts I ask my clients to sign specifically say that we can substitute equal or greater parts if we need to service their systems. No matter what parts we use, we always stand behind them.

CHAPTER 21
NEVER REFER THE COMPLAINANT

N ow that we upgraded our computer network, it was time to upgrade our Internet connection as well. I wanted to use a cable modem. Because cable service was not installed in the building our office was located in, it would have cost between $1,200 and $1,600 to bring it into the building. That was the price quoted to me by our local cable provider.

The decision was simple; we would install a DSL line from our local telephone service provider. I ordered the line and requested that it be added to our fourth telephone line which we used as a fax line. This way it would not interfere with our regular lines.

"I would like to install the DSL on our fourth line which is 6996," I told the customer service representative. "Just one minute," was the response. "We are having a special promotion this month. If you order before the end of the month, you will receive

free installation and a $99 credit to offset the cost of your modem."
"Thank you. How long will it take to install the line?" I asked.
"About two to three weeks," was the reply. "We will notify you via
e-mail when it is on-line."

Two weeks later I received an e-mail from them informing
me that the line was active. Along with the e-mail was a 26-page
document informing me of my rights and responsibilities regarding
the DSL line. I started to read it and soon discovered that even a
Harvard lawyer would have trouble understanding it. To this day, I
have never read through it.

I called my computer consultants to install the software
and modem that we needed to set up my connection. Three days
later the technician was in my office to make the connection. After
spending over two hours, both on our network and talking to my
service provider, he discovered that the line was not connected.

The customer service representative said that the problem
was internal and that my line should be active by the following
week.

The invoice from my computer technician for the service
call was for $250.

The following Tuesday I received a telephone call and e-mail informing me that the DSL line was now active and with it was the same 26 page document I previously received. I immediately placed it in the circular file I kept under my desk.

The next day my computer consultant returned to complete the installation only to discover that the line was still not installed. I felt like a child who was given an ice cream cone without ice cream inside of it. Another $250 invoice!

I was frustrated and furious. I called the telephone company again. I was told that the problem was most likely in my internal wiring and if that was the case, there would be a charge to come out and fix it. "I am in the security and telephone installation business; there is nothing wrong with the wiring inside my office. I installed it myself and it has been tested. The problem is on your end," I replied. "You don't know that," was the answer. "Yes I do. There is no DSL tone on your incoming line," I countered. "I can have someone there on the 23rd." "That's two weeks from now." I was sure she could hear the anger in my voice. "Not acceptable," I said. "I have now been waiting over six weeks for something that should have been installed a month ago. Not to mention the $500 it already cost me to install my equipment." "That's the best I can do," she said. "We will see," I answered.

My next call was to the president of the company, who incidentally was a client and friend. I spoke to his secretary and was told that someone would be at my office the next day to repair the problem.

The very next day two technicians were at my office and spent that day and the next day trying to locate the problem. After tracing the lines from my office and back to theirs, they discovered that the problem was in their central office. It seemed that someone forgot to make the connection at the source.

The line was connected and has been trouble free since that time.

Fortunately for me, I had friends in high places. I shudder to think of the frustration that many other businesses go through trying to get out of the corporate quicksand.

I don't know what was reported back to customer service, but the following day I received a telephone call informing me that the company was crediting my account $500 for their error.

It had been over eight months since the DSL fiasco and I thought I had been through enough of their red tape until I started to sign a batch of checks my bookkeeper presented to me for my signature. I came across two checks for two separate telephone bills which we received. I questioned her about them. "One is for our telephone lines and the second is for the DSL line." "Why can't they just put it all on one invoice?" I asked. "I'll call them about it."

She dialed the business office number that was on the telephone bill, only to be escorted through a series of telephone prompts. After about three minutes she placed her phone on speaker and continued to do other work while waiting for someone to pick up on the other end. All during this time, we listened to music and an occasional voice that would say, "Please hold, your call is very important to us." Well if it is so important, pick up the phone.

A while later, I was standing by her desk while she was in another part of the office busy with something else, when a voice on the other end of the line said, "This is Mrs. Smith, how may I help you?" I picked up the handset while at the same time glancing at the LCD readout on the phone that said this call was 28 minutes long and said, "Mrs. Smith, I am calling about our DSL line." "Yes how can I help you?" "I would like to consolidate my bills so that everything is on one monthly bill." "I'm sorry, but you have the wrong office," she replied. "This is the number that is on my telephone bill to call with any problem," I said. "I know, but I'm in customer service, not billing. You have to call this other number, let me give it to you." "No," I said. "You have to call it for me. Do you realize I have tied up one of my business lines for almost one half-hour waiting for you to pick up; now you are going to give me another number to call that will probably tie-up my line for another half-hour." "I'm sorry," she said. "I'm not allowed to call it for you." "You are not calling it for me, you are calling it for you," I answered.

"What do you mean," she said. "You're in customer service, then do your job, I'm the customer. Call the right department, tell them I want to consolidate my bills and take care of it." " I can't do that." "You mean you won't do that," I replied. "I guess you don't care about your job. If enough of your customers tie-up their telephones trying to solve a problem that would probably only take about one minute, for as much time as I have, how many business calls would they have to miss and how much business do you think they would lose? After a while, if we all lose enough business, we will not need telephone lines anymore. If you lose enough customers, soon you won't have a job. So, do the first thing that you should have been taught in customer relations school. *Never refer the complainant, refer the complaint.* Call the right person for me and tell them that I have a problem. They can call me at their convenience and I am sure we can solve this problem in about one minute on the phone. Then I can go about my business and make money, so that I can pay my telephone bill and you can keep your job."

"I'm not allowed to do that, I can lose my job for breaking the rules," she said. "It doesn't matter," I replied. "If you keep working like this, you lose it anyway. Why don't you start a new policy; maybe more people will want to do business with you."

When my dad taught me to play baseball, I learned that if I caught a ground ball and couldn't make the out myself, throw it to the person that is going to finish the play. "It is the same in life son, if you take on a problem that you can't handle, find someone that can help you with it and get the job done. Life is a team effort," he would say.

It is no different in business. If you answer the telephone, you have elected to pick up that grounder. I don't care if you are the janitor or the CEO; take the information, pass it along to the right person, follow-up, make sure the problem is handled and score points with the customer.

CHAPTER 22
THE CHOCOLATE BAR

E arlier, I had mentioned the presentation folder that I used for sales presentations. The folder was one that I had purchased from a nationally known printing company. It was a heavy stock glossy folder. We had ordered the folders consistently every year in quantities of 500 each time. Whenever we received the order, it was the same as the first. The consistency was nice and we did not have to think about it. My office manager would just call the company, give them the reorder and we would have what we needed within ten days.

Sometime in early January of 2002, I realized we were running low on folders. With the home show coming up within the next four weeks, I wanted to be certain that we had enough presentation folders to hand out.

When the folders arrived, Mary started to make up the sales packages for the show. As she started to arrange the folders on a work table in the office, she said, "Something doesn't feel right with these folders." I walked back to where she was working and picked up one of the folders. "You're right," I said. "They are lighter than the ones we have; the stock is thinner," I added, as I compared it to one of the folders we still had from our last order. "Not only that, look at the color of the ink, it's not the same blue," she responded. "You're right," I answered. "I will call them and have them redo the order, they obviously made a mistake."

I placed a call to our company representative and explained the problem. He explained that the company had decided to change the folder slightly instead of passing along the increase in paper costs. In doing this, they would not have to raise the cost of the folder. You actually are paying the same price as your last order.

"I don't mind paying an increase," I countered. "I realize that the cost of materials and labor has gone up, but I just want what I have always ordered." "I do not believe they are using the heavier stock any more," was his answer.

"For the last ten or so years your company has helped me build an image by providing me with a product that made our sales brochures look powerful. If I use these folders you will be tearing down that image. This is something that I cannot live with," I stated.

"Let me see what I can do," he said with some understanding in his voice.

"I'll tell you what I am going to do," I replied. "I am going to put two presentation folders together and send them to you overnight. I want you to see for yourself what the difference is. Call me when you get them. Let me give you my cell number. I am usually out of the office and this way you can call me directly," I added. "I'll do that," he answered, "I will call you tomorrow, either way, I promise." "Thank you, I'll speak to you tomorrow."

I sent out two sales kits in the different folders by express mail.

The next afternoon, I was driving south on the Palisades Parkway when my cell phone rang. "Hello is this Mr. Solomon?" the voice on the other end asked. "Yes it is. Who is calling?" I asked. "This is Thomas from customer service. I received your package and you are absolutely right, the folders are like day and night, I see what you mean. Unfortunately, we no longer are using the heavier stock, even if you wanted to pay a premium for them, we don't have the material and as far as the ink color, that was a mistake. They printed it with neon blue instead of reflex blue. All

I can do is let you keep them at no charge." That doesn't do me any good," I answered. "I will not use them. They diminish my company image."

"Thomas, did you ever hear of the *Hershey Principle*," I asked. "No, what's that?" "It is simple," I said. "You don't raise the price of the candy bar; you just make it slightly smaller, small enough hoping that no one will realize it. When you multiply that small amount times millions of candy bars you save a lot of money. Most of the time, the customer does not notice the difference. In this case, you got caught." "I understand what you are saying," he said. "I wish there was something I could do for you, but unfortunately my hands are tied." "I'm sorry also," I said. "I don't blame you, I won't shoot the messenger, but your company just lost my printing business." I almost felt sorry for him. Thomas was most sincere. He really tried to help me, but was caught up in a corporate decision that he had no control over.

I showed the original folder we used to a local *Minuteman Press* printer who I knew, "Could you duplicate these for me?" "I'll have them for you in a week," he responded. The cost was less than ten percent more than I was paying my first supplier. Furthermore, there were no shipping charges as he was located just a mile away.

Minuteman Press is now printing all of our forms. The former printer had lost all of my business.

The one thing I have never done is reduce the quality of the equipment I use, even if I lowered my price. I would rather make a little less on the sale than have to send a service technician out two or three times to make corrections or repairs due to its inferiority.

CHAPTER 23
WHO WAS THAT MASKED MAN?

D on't get the impression that all is gloomy in Corporate America. There are many companies that truly do care about their customers. They have gone that extra mile. I have also had some very positive experiences. There are some companies that do not live by the Eleventh Commandment. When I am treated as though I am important to the person on the other end of the telephone, I find it refreshing. There really is hope, I keep telling myself.

My dad once told me that when you think things are really going bad, take a blank piece of paper; draw a line down the middle and on one side write good and mark the other bad. Then start listing all the good things that happened and list all the bad. The good will outweigh the bad almost every time.

I had trouble with a brand new laptop which I had purchased from Dell Computer. The hard drive failed and had to be replaced after owning it for less than one month. After their technician talked me through troubleshooting the problem with him over the telephone, and determined the drive was defective, he was most apologetic and said he would send me a new one overnight by Fed-Ex. He explained to me how to install it and gave me a 24 hour toll-free number to call, if I needed help.

I received the part in my office the next morning and brought it home with me to complete the repair. After I installed it and rebooted my computer, I found that my screen was absolutely blank. I checked my connections once again and rebooted the system, but to no avail.

It was about nine in the evening and I knew that their help line was available twenty-four hours a day, so I called the 800 number I was given. After a series of telephone prompts, which surprisingly lasted less than one minute, I was connected to a live female voice. "This is Veena, what product are you calling about?" "I have an Inspiron 8500," I answered. "What seems to be the problem?" I told her what had transpired when I tried to reboot the computer. "How old is your unit," she asked. "It is less than six weeks old." "That's the problem; you received a blank hard drive. You are going to have to load all of the information from the beginning. When they replace a hard drive with a new one, they do not load any programs on them. That is why you get all the discs with the system when you buy it," she added. "What do I do now?" I asked. "Do you have all the CD's that came with your laptop?" "Yes." "You just load the disc marked Windows XP into your drive and the rest is automatic. The screen will tell you what disc to load next. Just continue until you are finished, and then reboot your system and everything should be fine." I asked, "Are you going to stay on the line with me while I do this?" "No I cannot do that. The process will take about three to four hours." It occurred to me that I was going to have to stay up until at least two in the morning just to reload my hard drive. "Why didn't they load all the necessary information onto my drive before they sent it out?" I continued to ask. "Your system was custom built for you. If we did that it would take two days to get you the part. This way your downtime is less," was her answer. "I will call you back in three and one half-hours to see how you are doing." "Are you located on the West Coast?" I inquired. "No India." "In the Far East," I inquired. "Yes that's right."

"You mean you are going to call me at 1:30 A.M.?" "It's only 9:30 in the morning here." Somehow I felt leery about really getting a call back. "Let me give you my number," I said. "No need to, I have it right here. It comes up on my computer screen. Will you be at this number when I call?" "What is the number?" She read back my number to me. I was surprised that even in India, caller ID works.

Loading all of the programs was completed within a little over three hours. About twenty minutes after that, the phone rang.

I was shocked. I really didn't expect a call back and especially surprised that it was on time. "Hello, is this Mr. Solomon?" "Yes." "This is Veena. How did everything work out?" "Very well," I said. "Do you have backups of all of your files?" "Yes I do." "You know that now that you installed your programs, you will have to reload your files," she stated. "Yes, I know." "Okay, if you do not need anything else I will say goodbye. Please call back if you run into any other problems." "Thank you, good night."

I was really stunned. Even though I truly believed that Dell should have loaded all the programs prior to sending out the new hard drive, the way they handled it was terrific. What I was really annoyed about was the time. It was nearly 2:00 A.M. and I had to be up at six for work. That wasn't their fault; it was I who decided to call them in the late evening. What was nice is that they were there.

Recently, I moved into my new home. I called Adelphia, my local cable TV provider, to connect my service. When the technician arrived at his appointed time, he discovered that the underground wiring from the street to my house was either missing or buried and they would have to rerun the connection. He stated that he would not be able to do it at that time because the wire must pass under my driveway. They would have to use a special drill to run the wire under my driveway without disturbing the pavement. (The drill that is used is a large piece of machinery that is mounted on a trailer.

It takes two people to operate it.) The installation could not take place that day, but he would have it scheduled as soon as possible. "Someone will call you within a day or two to set up an appointment," the technician said. He further stated that he could run a wire across my walkway to give me temporary service that day, but that I would have to sign a form absolving them of any liability if anyone tripped over it. "That wouldn't be necessary; I could wait a few more days." I didn't want the possibility of someone falling and getting hurt on my property nor did I want the liability. My home was new and we had workers coming and going all day long.

"I am not a big TV watcher," I said. What I really wanted to set up were my computers. I was also using Adelphia as my Internet provider. "I'll see what I could do to expedite it," he stated.

The next morning I received a call from their customer service department informing me that they would have a crew at my home on Thursday between 8:00 A.M. and 11:00 A.M., which was two days later. The person on the telephone said that I didn't have to be home. She also stated that they would have their installer come back out to finish the connection. "That won't be necessary; when he was here the first time he installed everything that needed to be done. All we need to do now is plug it in. If I have a problem after they make the connection, I will call you back," I replied. "Okay, Mr. Solomon, if you need anything at all don't hesitate to call." She was polite, courteous and most sincere.

Thursday morning the connection was made and everything worked as it was supposed to. I installed the network for my computers, set up my e-mail and programmed my television sets.

I then called Adelphia's customer service department once more to thank them for a job well done. I asked for a supervisor. A woman answered the telephone and introduced herself as Diane. She asked how she could help me. I told her that I wanted to compliment her on the way her people handled my problem. "Please thank them for me. I have been in a service business for twenty years and it is nice to get a complimentary call once in a while. Enough people scream and yell because they think that 'The squeaky wheel gets all the oil'; it used to be that way but not necessarily anymore." I said, my dad taught me a long time ago, "You get more with honey than you do with vinegar." If you're nice, most people will be nice right back. Diane said she appreciated the call and if I needed any further assistance to please call her back. She gave me her extension number and further said not to hesitate to call her directly if I have any other problem. I thanked her and hung up.

You may be thinking that I just got lucky; it doesn't always work that way. Well you are wrong.

About six weeks later, my landscaper was replacing a tree and accidentally cut through the cable line that was installed when they initially connected my service. He was extremely apologetic.

"I didn't know it was there," he said. "They had to run it that way because it was installed after the fact," I told him. "Don't worry about it, it wasn't your fault." I called the cable company once again. This time I dialed Diane's extension. When she answered the telephone, I reminded her of when we had previously spoken and explained to her what had happened. She asked me to hold on for a little while, and then came back on the line about two minutes later to explain that she was trying to get a dispatcher on the line to ascertain if they had a repair truck in my area. I was on hold for about seven or eight minutes. During that period of time, she came back on the line twice more to make sure that she didn't lose the call and to assure me that she was still working on the problem. The last time she came back on the line, she said there was a truck working in my neighborhood and it should be at my house within the hour. She even gave me the technician's name. I thanked her once again and said goodbye.

Within twenty minutes, their repair truck was in my driveway. The repair was completed in less than ten minutes. I thanked the technician and tried to tip him. He emphatically refused, wished me luck in my new home and left. It was like a scene out of the Lone Ranger, "Who was that Masked Man?"

What amazed me even more was that Diane, the customer service supervisor, called my home later that afternoon to confirm whether or not the repair was satisfactorily completed.

When we moved into our new home, Barbara and I had contracted with a local electrician, Michael Gruber Electric to have some work done. It seemed that we would never get finished with the things we wanted to do. We kept finding more and more projects. Mike was contracted by us on three separate occasions. Every time he had an appointment with us to work on whatever the current project was he would call the night before to confirm the appointment. The next day, he would show up on time, complete what had to be done and leave. Except for the items he installed for us, you would never know he worked in our home. He reminded me of the way I ran my business. I told him time and time again that he was a breath of fresh air and that it was nice to meet a businessman that cared about his customers.

The last time he came to my home, he called the night before and said he would be there by 8:00 A.M. the next morning. He was going to install some additional outdoor lighting on our rear patio to better illuminate our pool.

The next morning, my doorbell rang at 8:15 A.M. When I answered the door and found Mike standing there, I jokingly said, "You are 15 minutes late, I don't know if I want you to start the job." "I'm not late," he said, "take a look out back." When I followed him around to the back of the house, his helper already had the old fixtures removed and was running the wire for the new ones. I said,

"Mike you amaze me, I can't trip you up if I wanted to." We both laughed.

It has always troubled me why some people think that when they call a company for service they start the conversation by yelling and screaming at the person who answers the telephone. You would think that it was their fault that the caller had the problem. Many times, no matter how nice a customer service representative is to a complainant, no matter how much they go out of their way to please someone, you cannot satisfy them.

I said earlier in this chapter that it is not always that the squeaky wheel gets the oil, but the following story is an exception to that rule. The situation was getting out of hand and the only way to resolve it was to give in to the customer. In this case, I was able to get some satisfaction out of it.

My secretary told me one of my clients needed to speak to me. When I picked up the phone the female voice on the other end of the line started yelling that her alarm system wasn't working and wanted someone at her house immediately. I asked her what the problem was. She said she could not set her alarm and that it was showing that something was open. I told her that if she would stop yelling, I would be able to understand her and help her resolve her problem. She finally calmed down. I asked her to go over to her control panel and press the status button to see what zone in her system was showing open. She said it was the windows in the front of her house. I advised her to check the windows and make sure that they were all closed. She was carrying a portable telephone, so I was able to speak to her as she walked through the house. "All my windows are closed; when can you have someone at my house?" I quickly looked at my service technician's schedule and said, "I can have someone there in two hours." "What do you mean two hours, I need someone here now." "All my technicians are busy, the first free appointment I have is 1:00. It's 11:15 now, if someone gets finished earlier I will have them go right to your house." She raised her voice once again. "That's not good enough, I want someone here now," she insisted. That is when it almost got ugly. I said, "You are lucky you are dealing with us. If you called the telephone company, it might take two days for them to show up." "Don't tell me I'm lucky, she screamed into the telephone. I pay you enough money each month. You get someone here right now."

I thought to myself that if she thinks she can own me for $20 a month, she is very much mistaken.

There wasn't anyway I was going to satisfy her. It didn't matter what I said or did. So I swallowed my pride and said, "I will tell you what I'm going to do. I will come over right now. I will be at your house in ten minutes, but if I find the problem is your fault, the service call will be $65." "What do you mean my fault," she asked. "You told me all of your windows and doors were closed tight. If

I find an open window or door the service charge applies. Do you want to check your zones again." "No, I know that they are closed," was her answer.

I left the office and drove the one and a half miles to her house. As I walked up the path to her front door, I noticed her powder room window was wide open. She answered the door; I walked in and said come with me, walked into her bathroom and closed the window. Her alarm showed ready. I told her the bill would be in the mail and walked out. I didn't say another word to her, I just left.

A week later, her husband called and wanted to know why he was billed. I explained the situation that occurred that day and explained to him how insistent his wife was. I also informed him that I told her before I came out what the service charge would be. "She said you were here less than five minutes." "That's right, Dr. Ballen, and when I come to your office and it takes you less than five minutes to draw my blood and you charge me $90, plus I get billed from the lab, that's okay." He paid the bill.

I am reminded of the joke about the homeowner who called a plumber to change a washer in his sink. The plumber told him that the price was $110. The homeowner said that his doctor didn't charge that much for an office visit. The plumber answered "Yes, I know, I used to be a doctor."

If Abe Lincoln was in customer service he might have said; you can please some of the people all of the time. You can please all of the people some of the time. But, you can't please all of the people all of the time. No matter how you try, now matter how nice you are, there is always going to be someone who, no matter what you do, will never be satisfied.

CHAPTER 24
THE DEPERSONALIZATION OF
CORPORATE AMERICA

It is becoming more and more apparent that there is an increase in employee absenteeism throughout large corporations. Much of this is due to illness caused by job stress. As companies downsize and increase their workload by multi-tasking employees, the expectations of corporate management may be pushing people to a breaking point.

The technological revolution that the world has gone through from the 80's through the 90's and crossing over into the new millennium has been so intense that it makes the industrial revolution look like a grain of sand on the beach.

The computer has taken the place of many functions in business today, sometimes to the detriment of both the employee and the employer.

I was checking in at Palm Beach International Airport for a flight back to New York. I simply walked up to a kiosk, slid my credit card through the slot, tapped a few choices on the computer screen and out popped my boarding pass. Since I didn't have any luggage to check, I didn't have to go anywhere but to the gate.

Glancing over to the ticket counter, I noticed four agents with no passengers at their positions. As a matter of fact, no one was at any counter, even though the terminal was busy. People were lined up at the kiosks.

I walked over and approached the closest agent. She was an attractive woman about forty years old with dark hair, wearing an airline uniform. "Can I help you?" she asked. "Yes," I replied, "but not with my flight. Let me ask you a question. Are you bored as a result of not many people having to come up to the counter for help with their reservations?" "You can say that again," she stated. "I must have looked at my watch at least five times in the last hour. I can't wait for the day to end," she added.

"How many people did you formerly see in an hour before they installed all of these computerized kiosks for E-Tickets?" "Usually about ten to fifteen; my day would fly by, pardon the pun; now it doesn't." "You must go home tired each day," I said. "That's an understatement. Not only that, we wonder who will be cut next; they don't need all of us here. Why do you ask?" She wanted to know what my motives were for questioning her. "I am writing a book on the negative side of computerizing corporations and I just realized as I was getting my boarding pass that the airline industry may be falling prey to what I am writing about," I answered.

"We had one girl get into a car accident. She was so tired at the end of her shift she fell asleep while driving home one day. Thank God she wasn't hurt badly. It could have been a lot worse." "I'm sorry to hear that; maybe if my book is read by enough of the right people someone may get the message." I wished her good luck and headed for my gate.

About five weeks later I was at Newark Liberty Airport. I was in the same situation, but at a different kiosk. I made it my business to see how many people were checking in at the counter. With the exception of a few people with luggage, only about one half of the agents were busy. I walked up to an empty counter to find the agent with her head facing down. When she realized that I was in front of her station, she put aside the crossword puzzle she was working on and asked if she could assist me. I asked her the same questions I had asked of the agent on my previous flight. Not surprisingly, I got almost the same answers.

I have since spoken to six additional agents at various airports and have received pretty much the same answers.

Here is an economic issue to consider. Previously, many travelers with carry-on luggage would see the skycap for curbside ticketing. Now, they use the kiosks or print their boarding pass at home on-line. Most passengers would tip the agent at least two dollars for that service. If that skycap services an average of ten less people per day, his tips would decrease by about five thousand dollars a year. Now that can hurt.

The airlines are encouraging and enticing the traveler to use their computers instead of making reservations over the telephone. They are giving incentives to passengers to book fares on-line by offering them cheaper airfare. Some will add an additional one thousand frequent flier miles to your account if you book through the Internet.

Today you can fly between any two cities in the United States without ever speaking to a single person that works for the airline until you get on the plane. If you didn't want a pillow or a drink you wouldn't have to speak to a flight attendant either.

I tried it on my last flight. I booked my ticket on-line and printed out my confirmation. The morning of my flight, I printed out my boarding pass at home over the internet and drove to the airport. After going through security, I walked to the departure gate, boarded the plane and found my own seat. If I didn't order a drink I would have never spoken to anyone in the two and a half-hour flight back to New York from West Palm Beach. Amazing isn't it.

Remember the British Air Commercial? "Where is everybody?".

It is happening on our highways as well. In the New York Metropolitan area, they call it EZ-Pass in Florida it's Sun Pass. I don't know what they call it in your state, but no matter what you call it, it is nothing more than driving past a toll booth with a transponder attached to your windshield or bumper to pay your tolls without even stopping. It was designed to help speed-up traffic and to lessen air pollution from a line of cars waiting at our nation's toll booths to pay a highway toll.

Does it speed-up traffic? Yes it does. Do I like it? "Absolutely." I have asked my wife many times as we approach a toll both and see cars lined up waiting for change, "Don't these people get the message?"

Most states require that you slow down to five, ten or fifteen miles per hour as you go through the automatic toll lanes. On some highways, you can drive through specific lanes at full speed and are not even required to slow down. Now the toll takers are standing in their toll booths with their arms folded watching cars speed by without even stopping. How boring and tiring not getting to say hello to a motorist as they wiz by.

One toll collector that I knew, who I will call Charlie, looked forward to seeing the same people every morning as they stopped to pay a toll on their way to work. It got to the point that he even knew some of their names. He said, "I was like a conductor on a railroad seeing the same passengers day in and day out. One driver would hand me a bagel when he passed through my booth. The driver said he picked up a dozen bagels for his office on his way to work every day. The people in the office wouldn't miss one. One particular morning he even had a container of coffee for me," he said.

So now, you prepay your tolls on a credit card and a computer deducts the toll due from the balance in your account while a camera takes a picture of your car as you drive past the collection area.

The problem arises when for one reason or another your transponder doesn't register properly. About a month later you get a bill in the mail with a picture of your car's rear or front bumper showing your license plate and listing the time and date you went through the toll. Besides the toll, they have added a twenty-five dollar toll evasion fee. The letter accompanying the invoice states that if you have a toll pass, record the account number on the invoice and include the appropriate toll and they will waive the penalty.

You must send them the toll. They won't debit your account even though that would be the simple and prudent thing to do.

I received one of these notices one day from the Garden State Parkway Commission in the State of New Jersey.

It wasn't worth my time or energy to go through my last months EZ-Pass statement to see if the thirty-five cent toll was, in fact, deducted from my account. I simply indicated my account number on the invoice and taped a dime and quarter to the invoice and mailed it away. Total cost to me was about one dollar when you add the stamp, envelope and toll together.

About three weeks later the State of New Jersey sent back my original invoice with the dime and quarter still attached. Along with it was a note that said, "We cannot accept cash, please send us a check or money order." I couldn't believe my eyes. I now have to write them a check for thirty-five cents. This was the most ridiculous thing I could have imagined. Total cost to me was now about two dollars. I suppose the total cost to the State of New Jersey to collect a thirty-five cent toll was about five dollars when you consider all the paperwork and payroll expense some clerk had expended. I wondered how many thirty-five cent tolls they spent five dollars on trying to collect.

I wonder if Charlie still gets his bagel in the morning.

When was the last time you spoke to a bank teller? You make deposits and withdrawals by using an Automatic Teller Machine (ATM). You pay your bills on-line. Your paychecks are direct deposited into your checking or savings account and your mortgage or any other recurring payments are made via Electronic Funds Transfer. A few years ago, I recall one bank trying to charge you to use a teller.

I recently needed some hardware for a project I was doing around my house. I went to my local Home Depot Store. After selecting the items needed, I proceeded to checkout. I never got to a register. There was a self checkout counter. All I had to do was scan my items and when I was finished, I selected the checkout box on the computer screen in front of me. It asked me what payment method I wanted to use, so I selected credit and swiped my card. I left the store and never even spoke to one single employee at the store.

Remember when you went to your local hardware store and you could buy one of each. If you needed just one screw you could buy one. Now everything is blister packed in multiple amounts. If you have ever tried to open one of those blister packages, good luck! I believe that they seal them that way so that you literally have to destroy them to get the contents out. Then try to return it when it is not in its original package.

I would not succumb to depersonalizing my business. People are getting more than tired of getting a computer to talk to instead of a person. Most of the time, if a person answered the telephone, you could conduct your business in less time than it would take to go through all of those telephone prompts.

One of the reasons they use computerized prompts is that they want to save employee downtime. It is a belief, that if you get the wrong person on the phone, you may have to tell your story to a person who has to pass you along to the right person anyway. So why waste their time listening to you when they can have you waste your time trying to press the right prompts hoping to get the right department. When you finally get the right department, all you get is voice mail because no one is there. So you leave your name and number and hopefully it is not days or weeks before they call you back.

I have never used a computerized message service in my business. I have always insisted on the personal, human touch. Even if you called my office at 2:00 A.M., for any reason whatsoever, you got a live person. They would answer the call before the third ring. If you needed help and it was of an emergency nature, you would get a call back from one of my technicians within ten minutes.

If you are in a people business, you should have people dealing with people, not machines.

CHAPTER 25
PERCEPTION

What you are or do is not necessarily how you are perceived. Perception has many faces. Dad taught me not only to be the best at whatever I do, but to "set yourself up higher than the next person by perceiving yourself to be different."

I am reminded of the story of three baseball empires arguing over the meaning of the word perception. The first one said, "There are balls and strikes and I call them as I see them." The second one said, "There are balls and strikes and I call them as they are." The third umpire simply explained that, "There are balls and strikes, but they aren't anything until I call them."

The way you perceive yourself in business, believe it or not, can make a large difference in whether you are successful or not.

Michael Solomon

Ask yourself what you do for a living. If you are a truck driver, what do you deliver? Food products for a major supermarket chain; well, if you think of yourself as a truck driver that's all you will ever be.

I am a cable splicer for my local telephone company. Okay, so you run wires to earn a living.

Well, think about this, that truck driver is responsible for seeing that people get a balanced meal and have food on their table to feed their families. The cable splicer is the person who keeps the lines of communications working as they should.

Do you see what I mean? It is how you perceive yourself that others start to perceive you as well. It is no different in business.

If you asked any of my competitors what business they were in, they would all tell you that they install alarm systems. From the day I went into business, when someone would ask me what I did, my answer was that I protect life and property. My entire staff has learned that lesson and has repeated it many times when people ask what we do. Not only that, a prospective client at a sales call is advised that this is what we do, protect their life and property. We may use alarm equipment to do it, but our first responsibility is to protect their life and property the way I would protect mine.

It has always amazed me that in many businesses, the way you present yourself can determine whether or not you are going to close a sale. I don't mean the way you dress for a sales presentation, although neatness does count, I mean the way you perceive your mission.

In any business you must have a mission statement. Mine was, *"Our Mission is to Make Your Life More Secure"*. This statement was printed in every copy of my newsletter and in all of our sales brochures. You must have a mission and you must believe in that mission and present yourself with that belief in your heart and soul.

The deeper your belief, the easier it will be for you to succeed; simply because you will start to automatically project that belief; doing this will make you more believable.

In my business, it sometimes amazed me how many people thought that we just installed burglar alarms. My mission statement made it very easy for them to overcome their beliefs. I would hear objections all the time. How you handle these objections could determine whether or not you were going to close a sale.

"I don't need a system, I have a dog." "We protect dogs," I would say. "Can your dog pick up the telephone and call the Fire Department if there was smoke in the house?" "I have plenty of insurance." "Call your insurance broker and ask him or her if they can replace your wedding photos or the heirlooms your parents passed down to you. I want to protect your home, as though it was mine and since fire protection is paramount to this installation and to me and my family, I wouldn't design your system any differently."

What I said, I believed with every fiber in my body and the homeowner knew it also. All that was left for the potential client to do was sign the contract and they usually did.

CHAPTER 26
MY CORPORATE PET PEEVES

I sometimes think that corporate America believes that Spanish is the primary language in America. If you don't believe me, read on.

Did you ever call a company and have a computerized recording answer the telephone? Of course you did, we all have. The first thing you will hear when the telephone is answered is, "Thank you for calling XYZ Company. To continue in English, press one." Whose country is this? Why should I have to make the choice? English is the language of America. What's wrong with, "If you don't speak English press one," then give them additional choices such as press two for Spanish, three for French, four for German, etc.

Don't you just love it when you go through about two or three minutes of telephone prompts; you finally get frustrated, press

"0" to get an operator, only to be told by some electronic voice that this is an unacceptable choice and it starts the original menu over again.

I called my doctor one day to set up an appointment; his answering system went through a series of prompts telling me to, "Press one for billing questions, two for test results, three for referrals, four to make an appointment, five for insurance questions and six for prescription renewals." The final announcement which should have been first said, "If this is a medical emergency, please hang up and dial 9-1-1."

Remember when you would dial the operator and a live person with a nice mannered voice would say, "This is the operator, how may I help you?" Now you have to go through about two minutes of telephone prompts just to make a calling card call.

How about the telemarketers, who when you answer the telephone, talk to you like they knew you all of their life.

Your secretary tells you that Mr. Jones is on the phone. He said it's urgent that he speaks to you about a very important matter. You're not sure who he is because you speak to so many different people during the day, so you take the call, only to find out he is trying to sell you the penny stock of the week.

Macy's Department Stores' managerial personnel wear white silk flowers on their lapels so that they are easily recognizable. I went to return something in Macy's one day. I approached a woman in a business suit wearing a white flower and asked her where I would go to return a purchase. She said, "I don't know I work in Customer Service." Well duh!!!

CHAPTER 27
NEW BEGINNINGS

B arbara had just gone through her second back surgery to repair two ruptured discs. I decided that after watching her suffer through another cold winter in New York, I wasn't going to let her go through it again. After much discussion and long thought, I decided to explore selling my business and moving to Florida where the warm weather would be good for her.

My monitoring service was willing to do my billing directly; it is a service that they readily provide. This way I would have an income stream.

The problem was finding a buyer for the installation and service portion of my business. At this point, we were billing over $650,000 in new installations and service calls annually. The new installations also were adding about 160 to 200 recurring revenue contracts for monitoring on an annual basis and it could only grow from there. I could not walk out on my employees who helped me become the success that I did. Secondly, I still had ongoing contracts with the building and construction industry to fulfill with a multitude of housing units that were still being constructed.

I needed to plant one more tree.

I decided to approach a competitor of mine, Earl Lorence, owner of Inter-County Alarms. In spite of the fact that we were competitors, we were also friends and had known each other for over fifteen years. His emphasis was mostly on the commercial side of the business and didn't do as much residential work as I did. His contact with the housing construction industry was limited.

If we were ever bidding on the same job, which was rare, we had the utmost of respect for one another. If a potential client told me that he was also making a sales presentation, my response was, that if I needed a system and wasn't in the business his company was the one I would call.

I still remember the day I was walking out of a new stationery store with a signed contract for the installation of a new system. As I left the store, I spotted Earl walking toward me. I said, "You're too late. I've got the contract here in my attaché case." He said, "Okay, let me go inside and at least say hello, then we can do lunch."

We sat in the local pizza restaurant and discussed everything but security for about twenty minutes, finished our slices, said our goodbyes with both of us sending regards to our respective spouses. We respected each other and knew that there was more than enough work for each of us without going after each others business. The respect we had for each other was something that was unheard of in our industry.

I knew that with my large residential customer base and his commercial clients it would be a perfect marriage. Now I had to sell the idea to him. I called Earl and asked him to meet me for lunch with his son Scott who was his partner. I said that I had an idea that could benefit both of us.

At lunch, I was prepared with a proprietary letter which we both signed and my financial statements for the last three years. I proposed that they take over the installation portion of my business for a negotiated price, which I would hold notes for. Included were 57 commercial fire alarm accounts that produced over $65,000 in annual recurring revenue. My central station could not service these accounts. These fire alarm systems had to be tied directly into our local fire department. They would get my inventory and my work in progress as well. They would have to service my accounts and retain my employees at their current salary and benefits for a minimum of one year. I would remain as an unpaid consultant for a period of one year. I was ready for any questions with regard to profitability. After all, the real proceeds in this industry are in the monthly recurring revenue.

I said, "Look at my financial statements. We are currently doing about $650,000 in new installations and service calls. Over the past five years we have been increasing that amount by about twenty percent a year. Let's subtract my salary, auto expense, perks and all the expenses related to the recurring revenue income and we would still be left with a gross profit margin of over forty percent. Let's not forget that the overhead also diminishes, you own your own building and I am renting. You also combine the insurance expense, your utility bills do not increase and you get to be me. That's the best part," I added.

"I don't know if I want to be you," Earl chuckled. "Why not? I'm younger, better looking and have more hair than you ." We both laughed.

They said they would like to discuss it with their attorney and accountant and would get back to me in a week. By the way, just in case you are curious, I paid for lunch.

We met again a week later. "Everything looks good," Earl said. "Our accountant said if these numbers are right, we can't lose. If we do this deal, your people have to stay in place." I said, "That's a given, they are the backbone of my business, they are my heroes, without them there is no way this company could run." We both agreed that if they were to buy the company that the name must remain and that it would be operated as a separate entity. They would be required to keep using my name for a minimum of five years.

"When would you like to close," was Earl's question. "Let's see, this is the middle of July how about September 1st ?" I replied. "I don't believe there would be any problem. Have your attorney draw up the contract and I'll alert my attorney," I added.

We closed on September 2nd, the first was the Labor Day holiday, and we physically combined our offices on October 1st. It took about a month to get things organized and running smoothly.

By the end of the year, they had recorded over $180,000 in new business and service that produced a gross profit of close to $45,000. They also hired two more employees.

On November 1st, Barbara and I moved to Florida to start a new beginning. I thought I was finally going to relax and start playing all the golf that I had missed over the past twenty years. Boy did I get a surprise, going from working 60 to 70 hours a week to zero is not easy. It seems my apple has a worm in it.

Time to go fishing.

CHAPTER 28
BACK TO BASICS

As I was writing this book, old feelings surfaced regarding the events you have just read about.

I felt angry when I spent almost thirty minutes on hold with the telephone company, only to be told by the person I was speaking to, that she couldn't help me because it was against the rules.

I felt cheated when the printing company was no longer going to give me the product I wanted that they were producing for me for over ten years. An arbitrary corporate decision to try to pass on an inferior product to their customers was something I wouldn't put up with.

And, I felt beaten trying to get the right shirts I wanted. If I let them try for a fifth time they would have probably gotten it wrong again.

So, where does Corporate America go from here? I have found that the small independent businessmen and women are emerging into the business world. They are becoming successful because they offer the one thing that large corporations cannot... *personal service;* that personal touch, which large companies do not provide.

Try calling Dell computer and asking for Michael Dell.

Give Microsoft a call and tell them that you would like to speak to Bill Gates because you are having trouble with Microsoft Word.

How about calling Michael Eisner at Disney because your hotel room was dirty or you got sick from something you ate at one of their parks.

Call any oil company and try to tell the president that you don't like the price of gasoline. You won't get past the operator; sorry I mean the telephone prompts.

In my introduction to this book, I said, "The executives at the top are so busy making the bottom line work to satisfy their stockholders that they have no idea how bad it can be."

So my challenge to Corporate America is this:

Bill Gates, one night a month sit down at one of your help desks and find out what your customers really want or need.

Michael Dell, take an order for a computer one day, build it and follow-up with the customer to see if everything is just the way they wanted it.

Michael Eisner wear a disguise, check into one of your theme park hotels, act like a tourist and survey the service personally.

When you visit your offices and facilities take the time to say hello to your employees; not just management: the secretaries, clerks even the people who sweep the floors. Ask them how they are doing. Show them that you really care about them. You may be surprised when they start to care back. When they start to care back the good feelings they have emanates all around them. It spreads like sunshine. It flows up through management to the top and it projects outward to your customers. When your customers speak to an employee who cares and feels good about themselves, they get the feeling doing business with you was the right choice. The last person I want to speak to is a customer service representative who sounds cranky and unhappy.

I can only mention a few corporate giants whose names come to mind. There are too many to list, it would fill another book. The rest of you know who you are and my challenge to you is the same.

These are just some examples of what is needed to get the humanness back into business.

Ladies and Gentlemen of the corporate world, your managers are going to tell you what they think you want to hear. If you want to make the bottom line better, listen to the people that make it happen; your customers and employees. Perhaps your new insights may help you to revise your customer service procedures.

There is an old saying about walking a mile in my shoes. Try walking in your customers' and employees' shoes someday.

So why not talk to your customers and employees once in a while. Using research questionnaires and focus groups are not always the best solution. They can be skewed.

Whenever I filled out a customer survey in a hotel or restaurant indicating that I was dissatisfied with the service or product I have never received a follow-up call or a letter. Does anyone even read these surveys? If they do, what are they doing about them? Thanking your customers for their feedback would be advantageous to your business. People would believe that you really care about them.

The only things that will make your bottom line increase are your customers.

Lose enough customers; you will lose a lot of business. Lose enough business; you may not have a job.

EPILOGUE

In February of 2002, Barbara and I flew to Daytona Beach, Florida to take my dad to the Mayo Clinic in Jacksonville for a lung biopsy.

It seemed that his forty years as a journeyman plumber, working with all of that asbestos, finally caught up with him.

He was diagnosed with "Mesothelioma", one of the deadliest cancers there is. The doctors said that he only had about six to eight months left.

We decided to move him back to New York to live out the rest of his days with us. There is no cure, so all we could do is make him comfortable. He could then be around his four grandchildren and six great grandchildren.

One month before his 84th birthday, on July 15, 2002, dad passed away, but he left me a legacy. The things he taught me about life and people cannot be learned in school.

During his eulogy, I spoke directly to my dad, as though he was a member of the congregation.

I said, "Dad, I don't have to tell you I love you, I have never failed to tell you time and time again. What I would like you to know is that there are over 150 people here, less than a handful have actually ever met you. I want to introduce them to you and tell them what you taught me, with the hope that they may teach it to their children.

Dad you taught me integrity by your actions as well as your words, you showed me that no matter what you do in life be the best that you can be at it. You taught me that being a good respected person is more important than being rich. You taught me that no matter how little you have, there is always someone else with less and you have to help your fellow man. You taught me to be charitable.

You showed me how to make lemonade from lemons, only you said if you get a rotten apple plant its seeds and grow a tree." With tears in my eyes, I added, "Dad, I didn't just plant a tree. Thanks to you I grew an orchard."

ACKNOWLEDGEMENTS

Writing any book is challenging and rewarding at best. Although it is the writer that puts the final words on paper, there are many people that help the author's work become a reality. I would like to thank the following people who have helped me tell my story.

Brenda Garretson, for her editorial guidance and support; thank you Brenda for dotting all of the I's, crossing all the T's and putting the comma's in the right place. Davida Rutrick for her gentle guidance in helping to smooth out the bumps along the way. Steven Klebanoff, who taught me that the hustle was not just a dance. Earl and Scott Lorence, thank you for allowing me to leave with dignity. To my daughters, Jennifer and Shari, for making me their hero. Finally, to my wife Barbara, a woman of valor, whose total support and brutal honesty made this book possible. You truly are my biggest fan.

ABOUT THE AUTHOR

Michael Solomon was born in the Bronx, New York in 1944. After graduating Christopher Columbus High School, he pursued a college education and at that time soon discovered school was not for him.

In 1966, he joined the NYC Police Department and had an extraordinary career that is outlined in his book. He is the recipient of 19 medals for meritorious and exceptional police work.

He has walked with Presidents, Monarchs, world leaders, the homeless and the meek. He treated them all the same, realizing that they all bleed red and put their pants on the same, one leg at a time. His belief is that all people are the same inside. They all have feelings and emotions, some are more fortunate than others. The less fortunate have to be helped, but most importantly their self-respect must be restored.

During his police career, he re-enrolled in college and completed not only his Bachelors Degree, Magna Cum Laude, in Behavioral Sciences from The New York Institute of Technology, but completed a Masters with Distinction in Public Administration, at Long Island University as well.

After 15 years of police work, Michael entered the corporate world of finance, management and sales. He became disillusioned after losing three positions within three years. He had a style of management that very few companies adhere to today. He was admired by his peers and subordinates, but not his corporate superiors. After much frustration, he struck out on his own and became one of the most successful small businesses in his field.

He was a member of the Board of Directors of IDT Venture Group, Inc. until its reorganization in 2002.

He currently is a member of the Board of Directors of Brand Aid Marketing, a public corporation.

He has written Guest Editorials for a national trade magazine and has also been the subject of numerous magazine and news articles.

After becoming successful, he returned to his old beliefs and started to take care of the less fortunate. His work for various charities with enthusiasm earned him the respect and praise of his community. In the year 2000, he was honored as Associate Man of the Year by the Rockland County, New York, Builder's Association. In 2003, he was honored as Humanitarian of the Year by Meals on Wheels and praised by the New York State Legislature in a Senate Resolution.

His hobbies include Golf, Traveling and Magic.

He is married to his wife Barbara. They have two daughters and four grandchildren. He currently lives in Florida and does business consulting and motivational speaking.

His story is one, which he was told by all that knew him, he must write, so now he has.

He can be reached at his website **www.successbydefault. com**, where you can pass on your own corporate horror stories.

Printed in the United States
30552LVS00001B/4-60